'across th

EDITED BY PAM SCHWEITZER

RESEARCH BY MAXINE O'REILLY AND PAM SCHWEITZER

PHOTOGRAPHY BY ALEX SCHWEITZER

FOREWORD BY THE MOST REVEREND EAMONN CASEY, BISHOP OF GALWAY

CONTRIBUTORS:

Molly Allsop, Michael Brazil, Jane Bruder, Pat Burke, Teresa Burke, Isolde Cazelet, Jim Cosgrave, Maira Curran, Mary Galvin, Julia Griffin, Bridie Hartigan, Kathleen Henry, Brigid Keenan, Molly Kennedy, Frank Lennon, Josie Machin, Mary Mason, Gerry McTague, John Munally, Thomas O'Donnell, Christina Pamment, Hannah Raynor, Kitty Thompson, Brian Watters, Teresa Watters.

'ACROSS THE IRISH SEA' IS PUBLISHED BY AGE EXCHANGE TO COINCIDE WITH THEIR THEATRE PRODUCTION OF A MUSICAL PLAY BY THE SAME NAME

Grateful thanks to the many other Irish pensioners who agreed to record their memories to inform our theatre show and publication.

Additional interviews by Gerardine McDermattroe, John Shergold, and Anna Griffiths.

Transcription by Dee Bourne, Christopher Downing, Anna Griffiths, Ann Lynch, Joyce Milan, Melanie Mousley, Lyn O'Hara, Maxine O'Reilly, Gerardine McDermattroe, Deborah Pearson, Helena Platt, Dora Schweitzer, John Shergold, Andy Soloman, Eileen Taylor.

IN LOVING MEMORY OF KITTY CUDDY, NEE MURRAY FROM COUNTY MAYO.

FOREWORD

Diocesan Office, The Cathedral, Galway.

I would like firstly to compliment those responsible for this publication. I'm sure it gave a great sense of worth to those who were interviewed. They would all seem to be people who had little affirmation during their life. To find that somebody was interested in their own personal life story must have given them great affirmation.

I always find it fascinating to read a person's life-story as told in their own simple style and words. Real life is far more interesting than fiction. It is 'for real' and therefore helps us to understand the mystery that is 'life'. It is in a certain sense, sacred as it reveals a unique and a valid expression of God's creative work.

Their stories also give a unique insight into the social conditions of their lives in Ireland. For instance, one gets a very clear picture of the hardship which ordinary Irish working people, whether rural or urban, experienced in the 1930s. There was seldom enough to go round-one of the writers mentioned that she never wore a new garment until she went out to work.

It also gives us the human story of the individual emigrant of that period and it is a story that reflects greatly on them. On the one hand so many of them expressed gratitude for the opportunity to work for a day's pay in Britain and yet none of them has had a hard word to say for the country of their birth or for the fact that it did-in a sense-reject them. Again they felt a great sense of achievement in having survived in what was to them an alien environment and yet they mostly appear to have hung on to the values which they brought with them from Ireland and to have maintained an interest in the culture from which they sprang.

Most important of all, at a time when emigration is sadly with us again, it gives us a very important insight into the effect of forced emigration on people. One cannot escape the impression of great loneliness and sadness. For me, the overwhelming feeling from reading these manuscripts is one of regret and loss as expressed so feelingly, if often unknowingly, by the authors. The clear message is that forced emigration is a painful experience. This is a lesson that needs to be emphasised time and time again. This manuscript should be compulsory reading for all concerned with emigration.

Eamonn Casey   Bishop of Galway

Chairman of the Irish Catholic Bishops for Emigration

MOLLY ALLSOP

I was born in 1908, and I come from Fermoy in County Cork. I didn't have a good education, because every time my mother had a baby, me being the oldest girl, I had to stop home and help to look after the family. There were six brothers and six sisters. I'd do the scrubbing and the cleaning and the cooking. My father always said, 'Molly, you were the only one that didn't get a good education because anytime there was an addition to the family, you lost twelve months of your school.'

Fermoy was a garrison town, and we had no end of British soldiers there. We used to go and pick up washing in a basket and bring it out. My mother would wash it and we'd iron it and darn it and put it in a bundle, put their name and the amount of money on it and take it back. We got tenpence a bundle. That was the only work in Ireland. I never had a job there otherwise. There was no work in Ireland for anyone at that time. When I came over here, it was a case of having to. An aunt of mine in Ireland who I used to sit with in the afternoons, read the advertisement in the paper and she wrote away and I got the job. She gave me all sorts of good advice when I was coming away. Oh I couldn't get away quick enough you know.

My father said, 'I can't see you stopping in London, not for long. I'll give you three months, no I won't even give you that. Don't forget you've got a home. You don't have to stop there if you don't like it. Just send word over and we'll bring you back. If you haven't got your fare, we'll send you your fare. We'll get it for you.' But I was hoping it would be permanent. I was hoping to make a home here and I didn't want to let the old man down because he was too good a man for that.

Molly aged fifteen is standing on the left

I came over on the 29th September, 1929 and I was twenty. I was going into service. The lady I was going to work for met me at Paddington. I had to wear a blue rosette and she wore a yellow one. If that train could have turned round again, I'd have got on it and went back home to Ireland.

It was a very big old house at Station Approach, Kew Gardens. I was working for an old lady and her daughter. The old lady was practically bed-ridden and her daughter had a business up in town. There was an old house keeper who used to come in now and again, but other than that, I was totally on my own. I was very lonely. If the housekeeper made some cakes, you weren't allowed to touch one. At home in Ireland of course you helped yourself. The milkman came one morning and I gave him a cup of tea and cake and I nearly got the sack over it you see. Oh it was a terrible big difference. When I first went there, I wouldn't think anything of going into the dining room and chatting. Well, that had to go. I had to stop all that.

I was up from six in the morning until twelve at night. I had a little attic bedroom with a tiny chest of drawers, a little mirror, a single bed and nothing else. I had to have a morning uniform and an afternoon uniform. Well it was very nice to have a uniform. I thought it was very smart. I never had one in my life before that and I did respect the uniform.

When I got up in the early morning, my first job was to clean the boiler and set light to it. They didn't keep the fires raging all night. Then you'd prepare the breakfast table, and get the fire lighting in the dining room. When the breakfast was over, you done the washing up. Then at that time, you didn't have hoovers. You had to go on your hands and knees to do the carpets. You'd sprinkle tea leaves on the carpets and then go at them with a dustpan and brush. That was their idea of how it should be done and I thought it was very hard work.

Then the next thing was to go and clean the front door step. I was very proud of my doorstep. It had a big brass panel and I used to clean that panel twice a day. I used to love to see it clean. Mrs. Salmon, the lady I worked for, was a woman who never gave you praise. She wouldn't appreciate what I did at all, and I was very choked. I thought, 'I'm not doing that any more', but I still done it all the same. I used to sing at my work. I was a bit of a singer in those days, and they used to hear me down in Kew Gardens, but she stopped that. Sometimes I'd go out and talk to the Irish workers on the road. They'd be out doing a lot of work there. Somebody on the other side of the road saw me and told Mrs. Salmon. She told me I wasn't to go outside that door while they were out there. Oh she was very strict.

I had a bit of a temper but I lost it all. I think you get cowed down when you're in service. It's all, 'You mustn't do this and you can't do that.' I'd find two and sixpence somewhere or a shilling. I left that where it was. 'Whatever you do', my father had said before I left, 'I'm not saying you're lighthanded, but whatever you do, leave it. They'll try you out you see.' He was right. If the old lady bought any biscuits, they were all counted and put in a tin. I wouldn't touch one.

I used to do all the washing there, sheets, damask table cloths, and of course they didn't have any washing machines. And then when the family came downstairs in the morning, I started dusting and cleaning their bedrooms. Then I'd come down and prepare for lunch.

I'll tell you a story. One day when I hadn't been there long, they asked me to do the vegetables for their lunch. They bought in some runner beans. And before they took them to the table, someone took up the vegetable dish and said, 'Where are the beans?' I said, 'They're in there.' She said, 'They're not the beans, they're only the seeds.' And what I had done, I had thrown the beans away, and there were these half a dozen little beans in this great big tureen. They took it very well, you know, they just said, 'Typical Irish.' I didn't know what a runner bean was.

When they'd finished lunch, you washed up and changed yourself for the afternoon, putting on a black dress, a little white pinny and a cap. And then they'd have a cup of tea and something nice for tea time and then dinner goes on at eight o'clock at night time. You'd hardly have that finished and washed up and eat your own meal, before it was time for bed. I earned my money there really.

I got fifteen shillings a week. I used to send my father half a crown a week for his tobacco, and I used to give my mother a half crown for herself. My father didn't want anything off us as long as we kept ourselves the way we were brought up and didn't get ourselves into trouble, but I did send mum and dad that little bit. It wasn't much, but it was a little help you know. I used to go to jumble sales and I'd buy a lot of second hand stuff to send over to my mother for the younger children, and some very nice woollies for my mother.

I think I missed my freedom most of all. When you're working in a place for a living, you've got to abide by their times. You can't just down tools and go off. You can't just say, 'I'm going off for a couple of hours.' Anyway, I had nowhere to go on my afternoons off. I'd go and sit on the common on my own. I didn't make friends at all outside the job. You don't get a chance to when you're working for these real old fashioned people. They didn't believe in that at all. I think they were worried in case I'd go off the rails and they were responsible for me, bringing me over from Ireland, you see.

I wasn't very happy there but I had to put up with it. It was a job. I wasn't going back to Ireland. I knew I'd nothing to go back for, only give them more worry over there you see. I would see no-one all day. I'd always be doing jobs, and then at nightime, when the housework was done, I'd go up to my room, and I'd be on my own. I often used to think, 'I wish I could see my mother. I missed my family, but I didn't write back and tell them I was unhappy. They had enough worries, so I couldn't really. But in the mornings I didn't want to wake up. I cried and cried and cried. The times I was going to run away, but then I had nowhere to run to. I would never advise anyone to come over here and go into service like that. When you are living in, you are at everyone's beck and call, from early morning until late at night.

I was determined to get out, but I didn't want to leave until I got something else. Well, it was a help when I found the church. I used to get up there once a week for seven-thirty mass on Sunday morning. I spoke to an Irish girl I knew there, Molly Foley, and she said, 'Well there's no reason to stop there. We've got a spare room. We can put you up.' So I came out and I stopped at Molly's and I got a job in a guest house in Warwick Road. There were lots of people coming and going there, different boarders, and I was getting rooms ready for them, always on the go. That suited me a lot better, and I didn't have time to stop and think. It was better because my mind didn't wander back so much to my family.

When I was in Warwick Road, there was a vicar stopping there, who was a very kind man. When he died, his daughter brought me up two of his suits to send home for my father. So I sent them home. I sent one first and I said, 'If it fits, I'll send the other one.' It fitted great and they wrote to me to send the other one. She brought me over shirts, beautiful socks, underwear and I sent them all home. It made my father very proud.

After I'd been in England a couple of years, a friend from Ireland came to live in Battersea, and I used to go to her on my afternoon off and every other Sunday. It was like being at home among my own people. She married an Englishman, and I met her husband's brother Charlie. And we were going together for six years. We had to wait until he got a steady job, and then we got married. He was a cockney and he was a good husband to me. He loved his children and he loved Ireland.

Every two years we used to go to Ireland. He used to go salmon fishing with my brothers and they'd go out at six in the morning and they'd come back with trout and he'd say, 'I want that for my breakfast.' We used to go out in the fields in the morning and come home with a big bag of mushrooms, and have them for our breakfast. We usen't to fry them. We used to stand them on the old kitchener with salt all around the stems. You could smell them a mile away, cooking on the hot range, and they were very good. Charlie loved the life over there. He died seven years ago. I'm now eighty-one, so I'm sixty years over here. It's suprising when when you sit down and relive your life. I sit down in my living room at home in my rocking chair, I picture my husband sitting beside me, and I go back over it all.

MICHAEL BRAZIL

I was born in 1918 in Waterford. I was raised in Waterford City. One of my earliest memories is of the big treat we had once a year. My Aunt Nell, my mother's sister who was in England working as a railway hotel manageress, for came over once a year for her holidays. A big treat was to meet her at Waterford Station and get on to a jaunting car. You climbed up on it and there were two seats on each side, and it held about eight people altogether. Sometimes you could sit with the driver and hold the reins of the horse, and you were miles up in the air. We used to ride home from the station with Aunt Nell in the jaunting car, and I used to dream of this for weeks and weeks.

She then took us on an outing to Tramore and we had a cream tea at the Majestic Hotel, which was the highlight of the year. We'd have our faces scrubbed and shiny. When you got your plate of cakes, there was some plain and some very nice ones, a mixture. And of course, my sister and I would dive in for the nicest of them, and now and again there used to be a bit of a fight, and my mother used to give us a clatter.

Christmas was another highlight. For a month before, my mother used to threaten us. If there was the slightest misdemeanour, Father Christmas would pass us by. We were good as angels, of course, went to bed when you were told to go to bed and everything else. Oh yes we believed in Santa Claus.

We had to put up our stocking and write down our wishes, which we never got, of course. We thought of things like bicycles and very extravagant things, and Santa Claus used to leave us a note to say that he was right out of bicycles, or whatever we asked for, but we still had a mouth organ, or had some money left, or whatever, and a bag of sweets.

9

We played in the street as children. A motor car was something rare then, it was mainly horses and carts and messenger boys on bicycles. It was quite safe because if a car had been coming you'd hear it banging and crashing in the distance. We played football, cricket, hide-and-seek, all sorts of exotic games up and down those streets. We had no fields near us, so we had to play football somewhere, but we had to dodge the police. They'd sneak up and jump out and try to grab us. I was terrified when I got caught. I thought I'd go to the gallows. There were about thirty of us out there, but the others all scattered.

I once took a vicious kick one day, and the ball disappeared through the front window of Mrs. Hennessey, one of our neighbours. There was a mighty crash of glass, and in about four seconds flat, the road was empty. We'd all gone down our little hiding holes, and the poor woman was knocking on all the doors. She never found out who did it, and of course nobody squealed. But it was very, very embarrassing. My own mother asked me if I did it, and I denied it with my life. We couldn't afford a proper football, so we made our own with a lot of rags and a stone in the middle, all tied together with plenty of string. They'd fall apart of course, and that was when the game finished. There were two kids up the road who were wealthy and they had a real football, but they were not allowed to play with us.

My father was a Seanachai, an old teller of stories. People of my father's generation, indeed going back long before, they have kept Irish folk lore alive, by word of mouth. Seanachai in the old days used to stay at houses in the country, and they would stay for a night, two nights, a week, as long as they wanted to stay. It was a privilege to have them. They'd not be paid for it, but they'd have their keep and they did nothing else but tell the stories. My father did not do it for a living, he was a civil servant, but he used to go round to all his friends and tell stories. And he told me lots of stories, and to a certain extent, he passed down the torch to me. He told me some nice stories, some sad stories, he'd spend an hour and a half telling a story. He'd tell ghost stories at night time, and he'd have the hair rise on our heads. He wanted the proper atmosphere with semi-darkness, for stories about selling one's soul to the devil and so on.

It is a tradition that has gradually died out, and this is why the Irish Folklore Commission several years ago sent tape recorders all over the country to get down those men's stories while they were still alive, to keep the culture alive. Perhaps after Independence, the stories were incorporated in school books and there wasn't the same need for these men.

Michael (front left) and his family

I have a lot of memories of my schooldays with the Christian Brothers. They were a religious order and they were very hard men indeed. Their psychology was to give you a pasting if you didn't know your lesson. You learned your lesson or you were crucified. In one of our classes we were standing around the blackboard doing algebraic cuts. The teacher would put up a sum, and we had to finish it off and to find a solution to it. The lad next to me, he and I were tricking and jostling each other, and the Brother turned round and caught me. He pulled me in and he hit me and banged my head against the board. I had the mark around my head as a souvenir of that incident. And he looked round for my companion in crime, and he couldn't identify him. We had to go, and we all sat down and there was a pool of water round this chap, just the sheer terror he worked himself into.

You'd go home and tell your father: 'I got clattered today by the Christian Brothers.' And he gave you a clatter, on the grounds that if you deserved to get it from the Christian Brothers, then he was going to give you another one, just to show you that, don't do it again, whatever you did, don't do it again.

The Christian Brothers were good teachers. I'm talking now about the 1930s, when I went to secondary school. Unemployment was absolutely rife in Ireland. There was a terror of poverty in those days. I've seen big grown up people with no shoes on them, genuine poverty. And there was no such thing as social security in those days. The Christian Brothers tried to get young men into the civil service, or the police, nice, safe, pensionable jobs like that which were for the elite. The Christian Brothers they had excellent results in their exams, so I suppose in one sense we should thank them for getting us to that stage.

The Brothers took vows like priests, but they were primarily a teaching order. Their sole job was to teach the young, and also to try to persuade us to become Christian Brothers in our turn. And of course to warn us of the perils that were waiting for a young man in the wide, wide world, especially women. One of women's main missions in life was to steer us young men and drag us down to their level, and open the gates of hell, and do all kinds of naughty things. We weren't sure what they were supposed to do, but we were terrified of girls. And we were warned to keep away from them. And I believe that the girls were warned by the nuns about us boys.

Naturally, when you were sixteen, seventeen you started getting strange feelings. And then, of course, the Brothers warned us about this without being all that explicit about it. But they told us the remedy was to soak ourselves in cold water, or go for a long run, and think nice thoughts, holy thoughts, or say three short quick prayers to banish this demon from our minds. Of course you never had sex education in those days. I think they told me at home that I was found under a ditch, or my sister was brought in the doctor's black bag, that kind of thing, you know.

If you wanted a date with a girl, first of all the big problem was circumventing your parents. Certainly everybody had to be home for half past nine every night, so there was no question of coming in at two o'clock in the morning. I would have been thrown out if I had. We were very lucky because there were plenty of little lanes, and byways, and highways, around Waterford where you could bring your girl, and you stood there with your hand on each other, occasionally snatching a quick kiss. Our lecherous pleasure was all very harmless.

There was a ritual, a very clearly defined ritual in those days. The boys never chased the girls; it was always vice-versa. If some girl fancied me, she didn't come up to me and say, 'I fancy you.' Her friend came to you, and said that, Mary or whatever her name was, was asking for you. The really important phrase was, 'Asking for you.' And this was thought of as the gateway to paradise when you were told that. Well one day, one of Mary's pals came to me and gave me the magic message, that Mary was asking for me. So it was up to you to bump into Mary accidently and sort of walk down the street after school with her, and maybe carry her bag or something, and then it was up to you if you wanted to take it from there then. But Mary was willing, shall we say. And that was it.

When I was eighteen I entered the Civil Service in Dublin. I then got a post in the Irish Embassy in London. I loved it. I wanted to come to London because it was a Mecca in everyone's life, to come to London. Especially when you came to a nice little post, a nice job, among your own colleagues, many of whom I knew beforehand anyway. And then London itself, of course, was a magnet.

I was only a week in London, when they took me to The Windmill Theatre. I kind of looked out in front of me in case somebody saw me going in there. There was a stage with naked women, and you know it was a very exciting sight to see naked women, I enjoyed it mind you. They had to pose, they had to stand absolutely stock still, and couldn't move. I made a point of getting to The Windmill, first thing, to see this.

One thing I did miss from Ireland was the colour green. I used to go round to all the football pitches, and places like Regents Park, and Hyde Park. And the grass wasn't as green as at home, I know that.

The accents of the people I found very, very funny, especially Cockney accents, dropping the H's and all that. No doubt they found my accent funny also. I'll tell you one little story. A good while ago I got a 'phone call from some old lady, she was down in Cornwall. She rang up to make some enquiry, and I gave her the answer in detail — I think something to do with her passport, or whatever — and the next thing that I heard was her sobbing on the 'phone. And I said, 'Is there anything wrong?' She said, 'I'm crying because I'm listening to your accent. It's so long ago since I heard an Irish accent. Do you mind if I cry?' I suppose down in Devon and Cornwall there's not that many Irish people down there. She was actually sobbing because she heard an Irish accent!

JANE BRUDER

I was born up the Wicklow Mountains, in 1900. We were farmers, and all it was at home was hard work and no money.

I didn't start school till I was eight. My father died in August 1908, and I didn't start school until after that. We had five and a half miles, Irish miles to go to school. There was a race from the time we left home to the time we went to the school door we never stopped running. I don't know what would happen if we were late. They'd come from there and there and there. From small farms all round. There was a crowd that came from right across the bog, three or four of them. They'd all come riding down on asses or donkeys. And of course at lunchtime we used to be all out on top of the donkeys.

Our teacher was Miss Tool and she had a great spot in her heart for our family because she had her eye on my uncle Dan. Miss Tool was a man and a woman bashed into one. Well she had to cope with big farming boys. They were hefty great lads and they took some managing. I remember one day getting into some tricks at my desk and she called for order and it didn't come. So she had an ash plant. She had a cane, an ordinary cane and she had an ash-plant as well. You know, swishy swishy. She went down to my desk and she said, 'I'll move the legs from under you.' And the desk fell over and I was all covered in ink.

If I went to school three days a week I was lucky. I wasn't kept at home from school because I had a pain in my head or toe, but because I'd got to take a horse or two to the forge. I had to work on the farm and I was outdoors doing a boy's work because my brothers, Bob and Bill, were away during the first world war. My brother Jim, who was only a year older than me was head of the house.

I wanted to get away from home because there was so much work for me to do and no relief and no money. I mean we girls worked in the yard and fed the horses and cleaned out the stables when they were out hunting. And we girls were never allowed to hunt. One reason was, if you get on a horse you must have a perfect outfit, and my mother couldn't afford an outfit for us girls (that was Bridget and me) but she did afford one for the boys. Oh yes. They were dressed to the waist and they were on the best horses.

Jane's brother with one of their horses

My oldest sister Babs was no horsewoman. She went into the confectionery business. My mother had to pay thirty pounds fee to Bowls of Richmond Sreet in Dublin, and she had to keep her for two years.

Well I wanted to get away from home too, so how did I manage it? Well it was a Whit Monday, and we went to a place by a waterfall, where we met the relations and friends from Dublin.

There was a big marquee and plenty to eat and dancing and music. And I met a distant cousin there, Bridie Wilson and she was matron of the Richmond Asylum in Dublin. So she said, 'How are you getting on Jane?' I said, 'I'm just peppering to get away from home, I must get away.' She said, 'What are you thinking of doing?' 'I'll do anything, I'd just do anything'.

Jane's father, 1907, a keen horseman

I knew a niece of hers May Short, who was nursing in the Richmond Asylum and she used to come and stay with us. She was a great sport and very friendly but we knew nothing about the background of Richmond Asylum. Jesus that was a dreadful place. So I said, 'Bridie, could you make room for me in your establishment?' 'Oh', she said, 'Jane you wouldn't like it, oh no you would not like it. Yes I guarantee you wouldn't like it.' 'Well', I said 'I'll chance it if you'll take me.' And she said, 'I'll send a form to your mother and you can fill in the form.' So the form came and I had to have two references. I asked the parish priest and Major Wensley. So I went on horseback to see Major Wensley first and ask him if he would be a referee. He said, 'Yes rather. I'll give you a good reference as a horsewoman! But I don't think you'll like it in the asylum.' So I said, 'I'm going anyway. If I can get in I'm going.'

So I went to the parish priest and he said similar, 'You won't like it. But Biddy Wilson will do out the best she can for you I know that. But I know you won't like it.'

Well anyway I was accepted. It was in 1919. Mother came with me and there was a man in uniform at the entrance gate, and all lovely flowers, lovely trees, lovely lawns, oh it looked lovely. Bridie was expecting us and she had tea for us and she and mother talked quite a bit. Then mother left and I cried day and night for three weeks.

Jane's family. Jane is seated front left.

The place was mad as hell. It was a mad house. There were no drugs of any description. There was one huge dining room for all these people, all as mad as hatters. They hadn't got cups and saucers, they had bowls and those bowls were flying here there and everywhere. I ran like hell. Got to my bedroom and cried cried cried.

At first I was put in with the ladies on ward 18, and a lot of them were far saner than I was. A lot of them were wealthy people, but they had no-one to claim them from home. And a lot of them had no family. Well Biddy put me there for to try and get me settled in. I just had to pacify them, but my ward was all right, they didn't want pacifying, they were all practically sane. Some of them were very aged and had been there for ages. For three weeks I was absolutely helpless, particularly going into the dining room. That frightened the life out of me. The patients had no treatment at all, except the straitjacket and the padded cell.

I was paid thirty shillings for one month, but we were fed and we were clothed. We'd have a uniform, I think it was blue and white, very attractive. And stockings and shoes were made on the premises, made by the patients, and of course the craftsman would be in charge of that.

Well time passed and I made friends with a girl from Sligo, her name was Finnigan and we were off at the same time so we used to go up the park.

Part of the asylum was given to the blue boys. The blue boys were the soldiers who were wounded and came over to Ireland to be nursed because Ireland was under England at the time. They had this wing, and we used to have concerts, teas, social evenings. Finnigan and I were always together so we got friendly with a couple of the boys and one of them said to me, 'How do you like it here?' I said, 'I don't like it at all'. He said, 'We've come from a wonderful hospital in Epsom called the Horton War Hospital. It's a marvellous hospital and you'd like it there.' I said, 'I'd like to go to Epsom because during the war my brother Bill was head man in Wooton's training stables, an overseer. Bill has told us you've never seen a horse until you get to Epsom, so I want to go and see the horses in Epsom.'

And things were pretty hot in Ireland at this time, in 1921. They were fighting amongst themselves and even the staff were fighting because they were on different sides. Bridie Wilson said to me, 'Now Jane I'm going to give you a bit of advice. On no consideration enter into politics or religion. When that stuff comes up . . . you keep clear.' So I did. I took her advice.

Well anyway one day, Finnigan and I we were on night duty and we were out on the town and we were coming up Henry Street and there was a lady and gentleman in front of us just walking and the man was shot dead right in front of us. And the man who shot him dashed across the road into an alleyway. So hell seemed to open up, the ambulance rushing in, and the Black and Tans were firing up in the air as they turned into Henry Street and the people were terrified. A lot of them were trying to get into the shops, get off the street and the cracking of glass with the weight of the bodies against the glass, the glass windows were breaking. Well anyway we kept moving, Finnigan and I, and we were getting along as best we could when we met this policeman. He said, 'Keep in girls, keep into the side but keep going.' So we kept in and kept going and we got home. We decided to say nothing at all, not a word, but we didn't go in for dinner before we went on night duty. Both of us were white. We were on different wards and during the night the patrol nurse came along and she said, 'Your friend Finnigan is not very well.' I said, 'Oh, what's the matter with her?' She said, 'I don't know.' So on the next round she came, she said, 'Finnigan's been taken to the infirmary and she's in a bad way. What did you do when you were out?'

'Oh,' I said, 'just the usual', in a casual way, 'just the usual.' And she said, 'Do you know there was shooting down the town? And Doctor Roberts' son was shot.'

Doctor Roberts was one of the head doctors in the Richmond Asylum, he was the second in command. It was his son that was shot. That's the one I saw being shot and so at the time I said nothing, then we learned who this man was and he was shot because he was working in the castle, in Dublin castle. So I thought to myself, 'here goes.' I wanted to get out. The incident had knocked the stuffing out of Finnigan, and it knocked me stiff too. I cleared as soon as I could.

I wrote straight away to the matron at the Horton War Hospital in Epsom. So the matron wrote back and said that it was no longer the Horton War Hospital, it had been turned over to its original state as a mental hospital. It's the Horton Mental Hospital. She enclosed an application form, and said, 'If you're interested, please fill it up and send it.' So I did and they contacted me by a letter to Bridie Wilson and I was called to the office. She didn't know about the incident we had seen, nobody knew, and she said to me, 'After putting up with you whinging and crying and sniffling and you're just manageable now and you're going to leave us. Well, you can go to England and go to hell.' And I intended to write back to her and tell her I've come to hell but it's not a bad place at all.

Jane says goodbye to her mother before leaving for England.

I went home to see mother before I came over. I'd saved up every penny that I earned, and I bought myself a beautiful tailor made blue suit, lovely cloth and a hobble skirt and I got a lovely little hat, tight fitting hat with a feather in it — I don't know what colour it was — so I had to go and see mother. She couldn't do anything, it was no good her stopping me going to England. She wasn't sorry because she knew, she had a feeling I wasn't happy in Richmond, and I don't think she was quite happy with me working there either. And she knew I wouldn't have stayed at home because there was nothing but hard work. So she came and saw me to the boat from Dun Laoghaire, it used to be Kingstown and said, 'Oh I'll ask someone to look after you and see you'll be all right.' It was a pretty rough crossing, but I didn't mind, I didn't mind, I was going. I was going away, so I didn't mind.

When I got to Epsom station I had sevenpence halfpenny in me pocket and I couldn't have a taxi up to the hospital. But my case was light and I got there. And they were the kindest people I ever met in Horton Mental Hospital. The kindest nurses, the kindest senior head nurses, they were all so kind, they were lovely people. Different all together from Richmond. As different as chalk and cheese. One was a mad house and the other was a hospital. You looked after the patients properly. They were properly treated. Some of them were charming people, charming. I liked them very much. They were treated like human beings. I was paid five pounds a month there and that was big money. And the nurses there were a jolly lot.

The first time I went to the Derby, I was on duty in the morning and was off after lunch, about half past one or two. You were always let out early if you were going to the Derby. Well, a little nurse from Waterford asked me was I going to the Derby, I said yes, and she could come along with me by all means. And so we ordered a taxi to be at the gate to take us to the Derby, because there wasn't much time to spare. The men at the gate said, 'Girls, you're wasting your time. The taxi men could not be bothered with you girls on Derby Day. You see that's their harvest, the Derby, the race season is the taxi men's harvest, taking the people up to the course.' I understood that very well, so off we went, to leg it to the race course. Going up the hill, a big van passed us, a big tea van delivering stuff to the race course on the grandstand. The driver said, 'Like a lift ladies?' I said, 'Yes please,' and so I was right up in this van. And the little nurse from Waterford she said, 'What would matron say if she saw you going in that van?' I said, 'Matron would be jolly glad to get a lift and she'd take it too. So you're not coming? Right oh', and off I went without her. And this tea van took me right into the grandstand, so

21

I had a great position. I'd got to get this money on for different girls in the hospital, so I was bustling through to get to a bookmaker and I remember the bookmaker said to a man, he said, 'Pass me up that young lady, before she kills herself or somebody else!' It was the year Humourous won the Derby cos I'd got money from the girls to put on and he won. I just got this money on. These bookmakers have cars that you stand on so I had a grandstand view from the top of the car.

There was a parade going down and there was Queen Mary and the young Prince Edward who is dead, and the Princess Royal and they paraded down to the paddock and then back.

I worked at the Horton Mental Hospital for three years and I went to three Derbys altogether.

PAT BURKE

I was born in 1918 in Kildorrery in County Cork. My father worked for a famous English family as a saddler. He looked after the horses, and he used to be a sort of jack of all trades as well. He'd often take the horses from one fair to another. He'd deliver the horses and then walk back, anything up to forty miles. This English family were very much in the racing business. They had masses of land, and one massive great house like a castle. They sold this off and went into Cork City. The new English people, Hodgins, that took over were what they call black protestants and they were very bitter. How we came to leave that place is a story on its own.

This Hodgins he used to go around on his big horse, and I'm not exaggerating when I say that if you were on the road and you didn't more or less climb up on the fence to let him and his horses by, he whipped you. I remember getting a crack of the whip. The IRA had burned down some of their property because they were involved in recruiting for the British Army round there. Well my father wouldn't have anything to do with this burning whatsoever, but all the families on the estate were identified more or less with the republican cause. Well in that area I think you'd travel a long way before you'd find an Irish born person that didn't have nationalist opinions.

Shortly after Hodgins took over, all the families that lived in tied houses were served with eviction notices. Well he came to our cottage on a Sunday morning and said, 'I'll be coming up this evening and I shall lock the house up. I want everything out, everything.' We had a bit of furniture and we placed it up against the flank wall of the house we were living in, until he gave us the order, 'Get that stuff away from the house.' So it lay along the side of the hedgerow waiting for someone to come and take it. It was absolutely pouring out with rain, but eventually my father managed to round up a horse and cart, and he ferried the bits of furniture and everything into a house in the main town which was Fermoy. I remember it just the same as if it was yesterday. I was just getting on for twelve years of age. My family talked and wept about it for years and years after.

Fermoy was a garrison town of about four or five thousand people. We moved into the house of a friend, and we were very happy there. It was vacant at the time and it was quite spacious. We stayed a number of years in Fermoy until I left school at sixteen.

My father was a very adaptable man. He immediately got a job from the council. He got a job because of his experience and all that. He was to go round repairing fences and putting up new ones as well. Once or twice a year they'd have a big grant from the government, to do tarring and re-surfacing of the roads. They'd take on extra staff as well for going along all the sides of the roads trimming the hedges and everything else. And cutting back along the sides of the footpaths, and all that.

I used to help out a wheelwright who made all sorts of stuff for local shops, counters, and everything else. I was always in there, helping out as a glue-pot boy. And we used to fit out the traps, bend the mudguards which had beautiful engravings on them to suit the family, with all beautiful gold embossed. People used these traps with little trotting horses for going driving round the country, for going off to Mass in the morning, because it was swanking if you had a good one. And they were lovely. You sat inside it, and they had three seats that way, and probably three that way, and a nice little door at the back with a step to get out of. There were different versions of it. And the mudguards were either side to stop the mud being thrown up at you. He used to make them then, and I used to help him out as well.

I had won a place to college, which was Saint Columbus College in Fermoy. It was mainly the upper class that managed to get there, because it was a fee paying college, and at that time it was pretty heavy fees. In today's money it was a pittance. But at that time it was probably the equivalent of the wages of my father for a month. Which was absolutely crippling.

The Christian Brothers, evidently, talked my father and mother out of it. They pointed out that it would be a big financial burden to my family if I went, because although I'd won a place, there's books and uniform to be paid for, and everything else, and that a boy could go out and earn his keep, be put to a trade. And they evidently talked my father and mother into thinking that it wasn't very wise to send me to college.

Even at the national school, you had to buy your books. I used to do a little private job after school, to pay for my books. I worked for a person who ran a gents' and boys' outfitters shop, a Mrs. Flynn, who had almost adopted me. I was terrific at Latin, and I used to teach Latin to her daughters while I was still at school. And on a Saturday, I'd be up to the shop and helping out there as well. People would come in to buy the bit of suiting, and then take it to a tailor. And you rolled it up for them, and very often enough you had to walk it round to their houses or get it on the bike and take it there.

Joe Green, a relative of ours, was the manager of the local garage, and my parents said, 'You go to Joe Green and you can be trained as a motor mechanic.' Well, I remember just as yesterday getting this big pair of brown overalls, and going off, and all my mates were saying, 'Good God, where's old Pat going?'

The head of the department came along when I'd been there a while, and said to me, 'How would you like to go over into the sales department?' That sold everything from bicycle parts to car parts, all motor spares. Well, I took that and before I knew where I was, I was doing nearly all the paper work there. So that was alright.

I had a girlfriend then, Nora Sitts. We were friends because we had so much in common. We were both Irish native speakers. And we used to go to what they call the Feis, like competitive festivals all around, and we used to win the cups, because we could tell stories in Irish. It was part of the drive to revive pride in the Irish language.

Very often we used to borrow the bicycles then, belonging to the people who had put their bicycles in for repair, probably on a Friday. They'd say, 'Oh we'll come back next week for them. We'll call in Monday or Tuesday for them.' And you had a big label on the bicycle, with all the details of what was to be done, and on the other side you'd got on what was done, and the time taken, like a worksheet. We'd take that label off, and I could get a bicycle, and I'd get a lady's bicycle out for Nora, other people's bicycles, which we were trying out.

There was one picture house in the town, and if the picture that was on there wasn't to our liking, Nora and I would jump on the bikes and go to Mitchelstown, which was about ten miles away to go to the next picture house. It was terrific uphill going on the way there, but it was great coming home. Once we were coming home with a whole crowd of people, and the Garda, that's the Irish police, had a big raid along the road. Anybody that didn't have lights, they knocked them off. I had a light, a carbide lamp, but it wouldn't work. It just got a bit damp, or something. So there was a whole crowd of us up at the court a week or two later, and we all got fined a shilling. I never paid the fine. I don't think anybody even troubled to collect it.

Funnily enough, when I went back to the town, about ten to twelve years after I left for England, there was a relative of mine in the local Garda, and we were reminiscing like we are now and he said to me, 'Pat, why don't you come and we'll have a look at the books?' So we went in, and he'd already sorted the books out, and he found out there was about twenty of us, in the books, that hadn't paid our shilling. So I paid my debts then.

Well, the first opportunity I got, I packed a few things in a bag and left for Britain. There was mixed feeling, with anybody that was leaving, at the time for Britain. Families were being broken up. We had a big family, we had five boys, and one girl. My elder brother had left, and my sister had left for England. My sister left for London just after she left school at fifteen. Well there was a recruiting system going on at the time for the hospitals, and also for people who wanted to go into domestic service.

She went to work for a family in Kilburn in 1936. She liked it and she got on very well. She was a real Londoner by the time I arrived in 1937, just before my eighteenth birthday. My elder brother, Jack was.living in Catford. He was a building worker, and they done all sorts of excavations, and he was a specialist timber man. He used to do timbering, shoring up and all that.

My brother took me out, on the Sunday morning after I arrived, and we went for a game of darts and a pint and I remember having my first drink in Lewisham, at the Joiner's Arms. The men there were talking about jobs and my brother's mate said, 'Oh, I'll get him to start down where we are.' Down at Blackwall Tunnel there was a massive engineering place called Delta Metal Works. That was where a lot of the building workers used to find jobs for the winter period when the building industry was slack. And I went along there on Monday morning and had an interview. I got the job right away and started next morning. And it was the end of the world to me, because of the noise and the heat from the furnaces and the red hot molten metal. I said, 'I'm not coming back here tomorrow.'

At that time, the people you worked with were so anti-Irish that you had to defend yourself everyday, physically and mentally. A week after I'd started, I was dipping steel rods in an acid tank to descale them, working with another chappy there. We were looking into the tank, and these blokes came along and shoved me from behind and my hand went into the acid bowl, and it nearly took every bit of skin off. And it was done purposely. I had to get medical treatment for it. Fortunately it healed up quite quickly, and there were no after-effects. They said I'd always have a very white skin, but it didn't seem any different to me. I knew who'd done it, and being young then, I thought, 'I'll have you.'

There was a system that you put your pile of stuff on one side for the bloke to come along and measure up and see how much you'd done. They had to find out how much they was going to pay you if you'd done extra, because it was piece work and a bonus system. So I put all our stuff on one side after I'd finished my shift, and when I got in next morning, I found that half of it was missing. So I said to my mate, 'Somebody's been at this.' I went up to the foreman, and I said, 'Look, half my stuff is gone. That's only half what we've done.'

One of the lads that was on another machine told me who had it, because he didn't like him either, and it was this same bloke. So I went over after this bloke, and I said, 'You've had some of my stuff over there, and I want it back.' He started shouting, 'Get out of it, you Irish bastard. Why don't you go back home?' And then all the other blokes, his mates, were joining in as well.

Well this bloke got hold of a load of sawdust in his hand and he threw it right up to my face. And I went for him, and I gave him the biggest hammering — I was never a fighter, or aggressive person — but I gave him the biggest hammering that he ever had. There was a big bundle going on there. And the foreman came along and he said, 'Out! No more about this.' So we all went up to see the chief. He said, 'You're all sacked. Out of it!'

So we all got the sack. A couple of days later, Joe Manning — which was the chap who got me the job there — he said, 'Oh, you can come back. The management realised who was at the bottom of all this trouble. If ever a bloke wanted a bloody hiding, it was that bloke.' They had no sympathy for this bloke.

On principle I went back to the Delta Metal Works then for a little while, but as the weather was getting better, all the building workers were leaving, so I thought, 'That's it, I'm off as well.' So after a couple of weeks I pulled out as well. When I was at home in Ireland I had a basic interest in joinery, of all sorts, so I started off with a building firm as an apprentice joiner, and I liked that, I really liked that.

Then 1939, the 1st of September, the alarms go off for the start of the war. I thought about it very carefully, and I thought, if Hitler was to invade Britain, we'd all be under the same jackboot. In an evil system all people suffer, Catholics as well as Jews, anybody at all different. And I thought, I'm not pulling out. I've had criticisms from my own brothers for joining the British forces.

You were approached after a while. You either took up war work, which is working in munitions, or maybe join one of the forces. You could even join the non-combatant forces, the medical corps or something. There were lots of people who were conscientious objectors. I was no conscientious objector, so I decided I'd go and join up. I had a particular liking for gunnery, so I joined the Royal Artillery. I had to do basic training with an infantry regiment, then you were transferred back to the regiment of your choice if there was a vacancy. So we done our basic training, which was with a regiment of the Royal Sussex, down at Ross-on-Wye, and after we'd passed out, I got transferred to the Royal Artillery.

I think every Irish boy in the forces had two or three English mates. The Irish boys brought a sense of laughter and singing, and there was great friendship and no bad feelings whatsoever. They all came in to fight the war, they were highly trained and they were accepted. And a lot of them got promoted within a short time. As matter of fact, our commanding officer, was a racehorse owner in Ireland. He came over and joined the British forces.

We were placed on the coastal defence up in East Anglia. We had a stretch of coast to look after from Cromer to Lowestoft, with Yarmouth as the centre point, and we had massive guns there: fifteen inch, 9·2, six inch guns, small arms and everything else there, to protect the coastline. When the invasion scare was over, we got trained in mobile field artillery. After a while, the commanding officer said to me one day, 'Look. You've been very efficient in the handling of guns. You passed your test quite quickly. You've been recommended to go away on a course to the College of Science.'

It was 1940. So off we go with a couple more to the Military College of Science in Stoke on Trent. It was a massive place there for gunnery of every description. I got a theoretical and practical training at the Military College of Science, and I became an Articifer, which entitles you to the rank and pay of sergeant. My job was to see that guns in the various platoons were properly maintained. You had four platoons, which was about twenty-five guns, and four or five spares. And you had to see that they were maintained and top notch all the time.

In 1942, I got married to Teresa. My brother was married to her sister, so that was how I I knew her. Our first daughter was born in 1945. I was stationed abroad when she was born, and she was fifteen months old before I saw her. All I knew of her before was a photograph.

We had landed in France on D-Day. That was the first day of the invasion, and we set up a bridgehead there. And the people we lost was something shocking. No matter what film you see, they could never tell you the real facts of war, and the horrors of war. Even now I have nightmares when I think about it, when I really think. Eventually we pushed the Gerry out, and we went on in then to the massive battle of Carne, and way up into Belgium and Holland, and into Germany.

Because I had been injured in a land mine explosion, I was sent to Stoke Mandeville for medical attention. My vision was impaired and I suffered then from what they call Facial Haemeatrophy. Everything down one side of my face went completely dead. And they worked hard on it there, and there were American doctors there as well. And the treatment was fantastic. It took the best part of six months, but they cured it.

Teresa came down to see me at Stoke Mandeville. Being young and not having had much married life together, she thought I was totally indifferent, that I didn't want to know her. I think I was very self-

Teresa and Pat Burke's wedding at St Saviour's Church in Lewisham.

conscious. I felt a bit of a freak, and there was something wrong in my attitude. I did feel hurt at the time, and maybe my attitude, or reception at the time wasn't right, but she was crying when she went home, and she thought I was a different chap altogether.

When I came out of the army, I went over to Ireland and had a good holiday. Teresa and I had great ideas about going to Canada. We chickened out in the end. There was too much involved, and then the second child, Brendan, was on the way as well, so it all frittered out.

After the war, if you wanted to re-establish yourself, there was a rehabilitation scheme. They would help. So I went along to the Rehabilitation Centre, and I said, 'I think I've decided to go back into the building industry.' The man said, 'There's a local refresher course in joinery.' So I said to him, 'Well, could I go a little bit higher than that? I'd like to go to the Worshipful Company of Carpenters and Joiners.' He told me to come and see him in a couple of days, but he didn't wait that long. He came round to my flat in Lewisham to see me, and said, 'Start Monday.' And this was Friday!

The work I was going to do there was a refresher course with a view to works management, drawings, theory and all the rest of it. They gave you a complete set of tools. To finish your rehabilitation course you had to do nine months at the training centre, and you had to do fourteen months with an employer before you came on the full rate. I could have gone out and got the full rate right away, but I thought, 'No, we'll do it the proper way.'

I started with a big London firm, Trollope & Colls. I was soon made a supervisor, and then general foreman. I worked for the big firms, Cubitts, Ashby Horner. The director there said to me, 'There are complaints about you. You are shouting and bawling about safety on the site. You are costing the firm a fortune.' I said, 'The accident rate is down and we're getting the job done. The factory inspectors were pleased too.' Well, the accident rate after the war was something shocking, it was a massacre, with everyone working on incentive and bonus schemes with a minimum of scaffolding and safety. But not with us. The director called me into the site office and said, 'We'd like you to take over the personnel, safety and insurance, and be based in the office.' So I did all the insurances for the cranes, hoists, negotiated with the police over road closures, travelled all over the country for them, building hospitals and everything else. I settled into that job, and did twenty-two years before I retired.

TERESA BURKE

I come from Ballinamore, County Leitrim. I was born in 1920. There was eleven of us, eight girls and three boys, and I was in the centre, between two boys. My father worked on the railway.

Before that he had been in charge of the saw mills, but in the time of troubles they burned the saw mills down. The saw mills were burned in about 1923. They say that children do not remember things, but I remember distinctly. My mother was in bed with the birth of my sister and I remember their coming rat-tat-tatting on the door. My older sister went to answer it. They were looking for my father because my father had two guns. One was single barrelled and one was double barrelled. That one belonged to my mother's brother that went to America, so my father took responsibility for it.

Those in authority knew that my father had the guns, because he had registered them and taken out a licence for them. So he was prepared to give up his own gun, but not his brother in law's gun for the simple reason that it had been left in his safekeeping and trust. The probable reason for burning the saw mills was sheer spite because he wouldn't give it up and they thought he had hidden it in the sawdust of the mill and they couldn't find it.

On that particular night — I can see my mother now, even after all those years, she was standing with a white nightgown on, she'd long hair and used to have it in a little roll at the back, but that night she had it plaited either side. She came out from the bedroom door, looking for my father, but my father wasn't there.

My mother was always afraid that we children would say something. They had a habit of asking children questions, as they might give the game away. Years afterwards I learned the reason my father was not home was because he had gone to collect a lifesaving medal. I think my mother was probably worried that he would have been celebrating and would have a little drink in. He had gone to collect his medal, and maybe they knew he was not home, as their intelligence was pretty good. Or she was afraid that he might come in while they were searching the house. We were fortunate as my grandfather had another house. Heaven knows what would have happened without that, my father now being without a job and with a large family, there were six of us then. We went to my grandfather's house and my father got a job on the Railway. He was an intelligent man and was good at engineering and so on, and because of that and being clerically minded and because he could do book keeping he managed to get on on the railway.

But at that time, your pay was more to do with the amount of service you'd done, rather than your ability, so he had to start from scratch again. After a certain number of years back on the railway, we came to Lauderdale Station. He got that because my mother was able to do the station mistress's job, so she did the book keeping and sold tickets, flagged trains and all that sort of thing. And we lived in the station house. I wasn't born there, but I have a sister and a brother who were.

We children all had our jobs to do. We all had to listen for the trains. We knew the regular times of the passenger trains, but there were specials. There were extra trains to transport cattle to markets and fairs and you always had to keep an ear out for them because you had to open the two large gates that went across the line on the main road to stop the traffic when the trains went by.

We had to walk three miles to school. An Irish mile is longer than a English mile, so it could well be nearly five English miles. We brought our lunch with us — a couple of slices of bread with jam and we usually got a drink at the convent, I went to a convent school, usually they would give us milk. There would be thirty or forty to a class. Sometimes the farmers' children didn't always come, but on the whole, as the nuns were very strict, they expected you to be there, unless you were very ill. We were all taught by nuns.

When I left school I had got the leaving certificate in about ten subjects. At that time we had to do subjects in both English and Irish. You were expected to do better in Gaelic. If you didn't do all that well in English it didn't matter quite so much, but they expected a high standard and give us a lot of poetry and reading.

> In Gaelic:
> Have you seen my little boy
> My heart's delight, my little Seamus
> He was going down the road to school
> He had no shoes on his feet
> Nor hat nor stockings
> My life, my heart's delight my little boy.

You'd be taught on Monday and be expected to know it by Friday. There were always exams on Friday. We have sat in a horse shoe, with the boys in one half of the circle and the girls in the other. You were questioned on memory, mental arithmetic and spelling and a recitation.

Before 1930 all the schooling was done in English, but when de Valera came into office he felt that a nation should have its own language.

When I left school I was hoping to be a librarian, and I passed the exam, but after all the worry and everything, I didn't get the job. I think probably it wasn't what you knew but who you knew, and somebody else who had a bigger clout got the job, which irritated me no end. I had passed for the scholarship to St Mells in Longford. The scholarship allowed me to have free tuition and free books, but not board. Because we lived on the station, and my mother being the Station Mistress, she could have got me a pass to travel on the railway because I wasn't earning, and if the train had come half an hour earlier I could have got a connection at Drummond and I wouldn't have needed the board and could have taken advantage of my scholarship.

I passed for entry to the Civil Service and I could have got into the Post office. I did get offered a job in the post office but my mother didn't know anything about that until I was over in England. After I was over here, Paddy Martin, the man that had the Post Office asked why Teresa was not taking up her position, and that was the first my mother knew of it!

My sister Betty was over here, and my mother found out that she was not too well after the birth of her baby. So my mother said to me, 'You go out and help Betty and then come back at Christmas.'

34

I think I wanted to leave Ireland because I read a lot and that encouraged me to think, and broaden my outlook. I had no intention of staying in England really. I would have liked to have gone to Australia or Canada. You don't look on it as emigration, but just that you want to find out about things.

It was 1937 and I was seventeen when I came to London and I soon got a job. I was lonesome and so on, but I was too proud to let them know at home that I had made a mistake, so I had to bury my pride and stay! I was terribly homesick, I really was.

I got a job as a parlourmaid in Blackheath at 4 The Orchard. That was a private house. At 4 The Orchard I was up at 7:00 in the morning. It was a living in job and my mother allowed me to stay for the simple reason that she felt that I'd have to behave myself, that I'd be fed and clothed and that.

Although a parlourmaid's job was not as hard work as some of the service jobs, you got up in the morning, you got the early morning tea trays ready. There were four different bedrooms you had to take them to, then down to lay for breakfast. You waited at table, then took the dishes back, washed them and the early morning tea things and the silver. Then you had to make the beds. You'd to see that the bathroom was clean, clean the silver, you laid for lunch and waited at lunch.

In the household there was no mother. There was the father, son and two daughters, and the father had an arm chair at the top of the table and the son, if he was at home, sat at the other end. You did not stay in the room all the time. There was a little side table and whoever was the eldest there, say it was the father, he carved from it. Sometimes it was one of the daughters that carved and you gave the meal to them. They didn't take any notice of you, it was like being a fly on the wall. They spoke quite freely in front of you and you were expected to keep it all confidential.

Looking back on it now you wonder why you didn't make more of an effort to have a better life, but the truth of the matter was that you were lucky to get a job if you were Irish. You were lucky to get into a respectable house. There were always jobs that you could get, but they were skivvy jobs. I knew my mother would never allow that, and neither would my sister, who was in nursing. To get a respectable job you had to hold back, you wouldn't dare let your feelings be known as to what you really thought or in any way fight for your rights as it were.

I could go and visit my sister on my half day, which started at about three in the afternoon. The father suffered from blood presure and often stayed in bed of a morning. He did a lot of writing and reading and that. They were chartered accountants in the City. And, as though it was on purpose, the very day when you wanted to be off early that was the day when he would either not finish his pudding, or he'd go backwards and forwards and still hadn't finished, and he would say, 'Could you bring me a cup of coffee?' or 'Change the water in the container', and you'd feel you could throw it at him! You had to hold all that back.

He liked quiet all the time, you couldn't even do a bit of singing, and there was no such thing as a wireless. Your only chance was when you brought the papers, the previous day's papers, you'd have a look at them, at least the headlines in the front, so you had an idea of what was happening.

I was lucky in my job, for the simple reason that the housekeeper really was a lovely person and I think she liked me because I was quiet and reserved. I was very shy at that time — nobody would think it now!

For wages we got about fifteen shillings a week, but you only got it once a month. About two pounds of that you sent home. We wore something like a nurse's uniform. You'd have maybe a check type of cotton frock, with short sleeves, a white apron, like a nurse's apron, with a bib and straps. It was difficult to provide the rest of your uniform for yourself. Draper Brothers in Lewisham was a wonderful shop, they kept a lot of cotton things. You'd buy one thing one month maybe and another next month. The people I worked for supplied the afternoon apron, which was a little frilly organza thing. I had three of them, otherwise you had to wash it at night so you had it ready for morning.

I did the ironing, and I'd dust the bedrooms, but they had a woman who came in to do the rough work and spring cleaning. Normally your day went on until about ten o'clock at night. I did have my own bedroom. I'd serve the supper but I didn't cook. On cook's day off she always left something that was more or less ready so that all you'd to do was bring it in.

My hair then was red-brownish. I think my sister cut it for me, I couldn't afford to have it cut anywhere else, and it went dead straight. I went to see one of the nuns when I was at home on holiday and she said, 'Oh Tessie! whatever have you done to your hair?' I used to have it long

HOUSE AND PARLOURMAIDS WANTED.

GOOD HOUSE PARLOURMAID REQUIRED; £30 per annum and comfortable situation; close to Portsmouth; good references essential; state age. Write Mrs. Briggs, The Hall, Gosport, Hants.   4 B

HOUSE PARLOURMAD—WANTED immediately, respectable young Girl, nice appearance; good testimonials essential; small family; three other maids kept.   Also good HOUSEMAID WANTED.   Apply Mrs. Garvey, Vevay House, Bray.   3 E

LONDON—Refined HOUSE PARLOURMAID, 23-26; lovely, modern house; light duties, no rough work; quiet, homely, family four; another Irish maid kept; wages 16/- weekly; send photo, particulars.—Mrs. Fox, 29 Dobree avenue, Willesden, London, N.W.10.

TALL, active, experienced HOUSEMAID and HOUSE PARLOURMAID WANTED immediately; £36, £40; send copies discharges.—D. G., 17 Beaufort Gardens, London, S.W.3.   1 D

WANTED, experienced young HOUSE PARLOUR-MAID, capable and trustworthy, with good papers, for small family; good outings, good wages.—Balholm, Shrewsbury road.   3 E

WANTED, experienced HOUSEMAID or HOUSE PARLOURMAID; send age, wages, copies.—D 1697, this office.   3 E

WANTED, 1st February, young PARLOURMAID, also good plain COOK; small family; near Downpatrick.—Box X, Eason's Advertising Service, Belfast.   3 C

WELL recommended country GIRL, with some experience, train HOUSE PARLOURMAID; Monkstown.—D 1774, this office.

WANTED urgently, a middle-aged HOUSEMAID (Protestant) for a gentleman in Tyrone; country situation; staff four; wages £36. Address "Z 3397, Housemaid," this office.   31 C

WANTED, experienced HOUSE PARLOURMAID, country; family 3; well recommended.—Miss Bigger, Falmore, Dundalk.   4 F where I could sit on it, and I had clipped it really tight and short and it had got dark. I said, 'It's no different other than that it's short.' But she said, 'Oh no, it was like the colour of Autumn leaves.'

On my half day, my sister would come and meet me in Lewisham and we'd go and look round the shops. My sister had a habit of looking at the boards in Lewisham, and on the posters it would say 'NO IRISH NEED APPLY'. There was a lot of anti-Irish feeling. It was so bad for the Irish lads that my sister rented a large house in Courthill Road in Lewisham. She had the ground floor and her brother in law stayed on the middle floor, but she let off the top floor to the Irish lads who were working in the building trade. They couldn't get anywhere to live. She didn't make a profit. But they had to pay their own gas and electric and get their own food. This was about 1938-39.

I remember once my sister coming when cook was off and I had to let her have my tea, because there was no way I would encroach. My tea was left over so I let her have it. I could not have taken any extra. There was another place where they actually did count the slices of bread. Another thing, you served the meal and you left the vegetables on the heat on the side, and it was only when they had finished and it was brought back into the kitchen and the dining room was cleared up that you could sit down and eat. So, unless the cook was good and heated it up, you ate it cold. There was only what was left, if it was something they liked and had gone pretty heavy on it, well bad luck!

On a Sunday at about seven o'clock I would be chasing across the Heath to go to church for seven fifteen, and then chase back again to be home to bring their tray to the bedroom for eight o'clock. You left on Sunday afternoon at three o'clock. There was an evening Benediction at six thirty, and you went from there to your Ceilidh, but you always had to leave by nine thirty to be back. I remember once, before I rang the bell I could hear the clock, there was a grandfather clock, and I could hear it strike but by the time they came to answer the door he said, 'You're late.' It was only about three minutes past ten. You couldn't have a boy friend because nobody would leave at nine thirty!

The Ceilidh was held in the church hall at St. Saviours in Lewisham. That was a purpose built hall. They always had a band, which was very good, and we danced all the dances, The Walls of Limerick, The Haymaker's Jig, The old time waltzes. You'd have step dancing and people singing. The band was semi-professional. It wasn't just amateurs, they were good at what they were doing. 'Danny Boy' would be the song that I think of. There were one or two very good singers and usually if a certain person sang, the response always was, 'Sing Danny Boy.' Another one would sing 'Bonny Mary of Argyle' but 'Danny Boy' and of course 'Faith of our Fathers' were the ones.

Faith of our fathers, holy faith
We will be true to thee till death
We will be true to thee till death
Our fathers still in prisons dark
But still in heart and conscience free
How great would be their children's faith
If they like them could die for Thee
Faith of our fathers, holy faith
We will be true to Thee till death.

It was just like a mini National Anthem, it was a bit political, and you had to stay neutral more or less. The soldiers song was sung, but not all the time. It was a means of giving us support. That was the only thing that kept us going, otherwise there would have been a revolution, the things we had to put up with.

When the war came, I went as a cashier into the ABC cafeteria. They didn't allow you to be in domestic service during the war. You either had to go into the services, or munitions or food.

I was at home in Ireland on holiday when war was declared, and one or two of the boys at home said, 'Ah well, now you'll have to stay, there's no going back.' That was the first week, but on the following Saturday, I decided to go back. I don't really know why. I think probably in the back of your mind you think, 'Oh well, you'd be a coward not to go back,' and I don't think anyone thought it would last as long as it did. There's a certain feeling in you when you're going that you have to experience life.

In 1942 I married. We were two sisters that married two brothers! We married during the war years. As a matter of fact we had great difficulty in even getting photographs, as there was a terrible restriction on. We had three large ones, six medium and postcard size and that was all we could have. We had to give the name and address of where to send them to. During the war, the letters we got from home had pieces cut out and some of them were blacked.

In 1945 I had a daughter, and in 1946 I had a son, so that was it for me, more or less. You looked on it that you had a family and your place was indoors. When the children were little and my parents were alive, I took them home every summer. I'd go maybe a week after the school broke up, and my husband would come for the last week to take us back.

As I've grown older and when my children left school, there was a terrible longing to go back to Ireland. But then as they grew older and got married, the grandchildren came, so you were more or less hooked. But I've given them strict instructions that I'm to be buried in Ireland, come what may. I've saved enough to take my remains back to Ireland. They may have to pay their own fare.

I think probably after the war, when we only had two children, we have four now, and they were young enough, say in 1946, and hadn't started school, we could maybe have gone to Canada. But the idea that if anything had happened, and we couldn't have come back, being on the other side of the world, stopped us. There was always that tie at home. Then, when the parents died, we still went home but it hadn't the same flavour. Because the family is seperated, Wicklow, Cork, Sligo. You see a lot of Ireland, and you'd love to stay. The reason I don't go to Ireland now is that, when I come back, it takes a month or more to settle again and I get so depressed and so homesick. My husband says to snap out of it, but it has such a bad effect on me that I feel I'd love to go, but I can't bear the pain when I come back.

ISOLDE CAZELET

When I was a schoolgirl, about fourteen years or so, I joined the Gate Theatre Acting School in Dublin, and I was in 'A Midsummer Nights Dream', playing the part of Mustard Seed, one of the fairies. After that I appeared in a play called 'The Drunkard, or Ten Nights in a Barroom.' It was one of those old-fashioned melodramas where the heroine is thrown out in the snow by the landlord because her mother could not afford the rent.

I never went on tour with that company, but when I was twenty, I managed to get a post with a small touring company, or 'fit up company' as they were called. Of course when I first started touring, I had no idea what it would be like, and I can remember I arrived at a station up in Donegal in three inch high heels. Now the station was a mile from the town, and I had a big suitcase, so I had to hobble along to a village. There I found my manager in bed with his wife and a great big alsatian and they were playing cards, in bed, in the middle of the afternoon! I was given a synopsis of the play I was to appear in, one never got a full script. The copy book just gave me my cues, and I found it very difficult to read the writing. I had to make up the lines most of the time. You managed as best you could, and there was a different play every night. You had a quick run-through where you were told the gist of the play, not the whole script. In the morning rehearsal, they'd just say, 'You come on here, you go off there', sort of thing. I remember when I was sharing digs with a woman who wouldn't stop talking, so I used to go and try to learn my lines under a hedge.

The company would all travel by lorry to the town where you were playing. The men would go into the theatre or small hall and fix up the

Shakespeare at the Gate Theatre, Dublin, 1936. Isolde is third from the left.

stage, while the women went around the town looking for digs, somewhere to stay for the week, knocking on hall doors. Once I had to go around on my own looking for digs, and I should add that one often looked very untidy, with lots of coats and headscarves on to keep warm, and the lady of the house said, 'Sorry, no peddlars', and I had to go away.

Local people were used to having the actors staying. They were always very friendly and nice to us all, willing to chance their arm and take us in. They gave us plenty of food. In the country, people usually had their own pig, or somebody nearby had one, so we usually had plenty of ham, huge plates of bacon, eggs, cabbage and potatoes, but not a great deal of fruit. The actors were given more than us, because men were supposed to eat more than women!

At that time the thatched cottages often had no toilet facilities or baths, and if one wanted to go to the toilet they would open the back door and say, 'The countryside is wide', and off one would go to the nearest bush or stable. Of course, washing was always difficult. There was one actor who used to put about ten shirts on, one on top of the other, never changed them, just a clean one on top each day. A great many people in the west of Ireland had relatives in America, and they would send back big bundles of American clothes, which we actors would buy off them.

A lot of the time we stayed in thatched cottages. They just had the open kitchen with the turf fire, and possibly two bedrooms. There would be a door at the front and back. Those places were never damp, because they had very thick walls and an enormous open fire, so they were quite warm. The turf was laid down on the floor of the open fire, and there was a hook hanging from the top of the chimney piece with a big pot on it. They used a number of pots, one was for making home-made bread, the cake or bread was put in the pot, and the lid put on, and hot turf put on the lid and underneath the pot, so it was like an oven. In some places there was a bellows under the floor, and to get the draught of air under the fire you turned the handle.

Very often, the hatching eggs were kept in the wooden dresser which had cupboards in the bottom, and the tiny live chickens would come out for little walks. There was one place that I was staying, where the woman of the house had a huge frying pan, about one and a half feet wide, but it had holes in it. Anyway when one would be cooking one had to tip it up, and some of the grease would leak out of the holes. Well those little chickens from the cupboard would make a wild rush to the grease, and one had to try not to cook the chickens as well as the eggs.

We stayed with all types of people, and I could tell you some stories about them. One place I stayed in down in the south, there was an old man, about seventy years, and very gnarled and twisted. He never took the slightest bit of notice of me, but would sit just spitting into the fire and smoking his pipe. It took me some time to realise that the young girl that gave me my meals was really his wife, she was just a schoolgirl, about seventeen or eighteen years. She used to go off to dances whenever she felt like it, and the old man did not like that at all. She told me that she had only married him to get a house of her own, but how she fared later on I do not know.

Another time, staying in an attic room full of cobwebs in Donegal, I came in one day and there were four or five great big fishermen with the landlady. She said to me, 'You don't mind sharing, do you? You're an actress, so I thought you wouldn't mind.' So I shared my attic. They had come from Clare Island, and arrived in once a month to buy their groceries, and then the next day they would go by boat back to the island.

In one digs, I had to ride a bicycle four and a half miles to the theatre, and riding back it was so dark that I couldn't ride the bicycle straight and I kept going into the ditch. There was another place, going towards the border, and I had to walk along there at night on my own. It had a clump of trees, and I hated walking there, it gave me a bad feeling. Later I discovered that some people had been shot there, years before.

One night I saw the Aurora Borealis, that is the northern lights from the Arctic. It was a wonderful sight, rather like a monstrance they use in the Catholic church. The whole sky was lit up with these pulsating fingers of light, and then it was gone. I had thought it was the light from the moon, and it was only when it was pitch dark again that I realised what I had seen.

People were very keen on theatre-going in those days, and they would ride on their bicycles from one town to another to see a play. The audiences really liked the heavy plays, with plenty of drama, no comedies. We did plays such as 'The Monkey's Paw', 'The Rising of the Moon', 'Maria Martin'. They were mainly melodramas, such as where the son goes away to America to earn his fortune, and while he is away, the bad son drives his mother into the workhouse. When the good son returns, he rescues his mother from the workhouse and it all ends happily.

The priest would usually run the hall, and often there were no dressing rooms, and we just changed at the side of the stage. In the early days we'd have oil lamps across the stage for lighting. They were inclined to throw great shadows on one's face, so you couldn't wear false eyelashes, or the shadows of them would be all down your cheeks!

If it was harvest time, the play would begin very late, maybe eleven o'clock, and the people who hadn't finished their farming work would come in late. Sometimes the audience was very noisy, and I remember one case where all the men stood at the back of the hall playing cards. Apart from the play, there would often be a raffle in the interval, and maybe varous 'turns' afterwards, where people sang or did a comedy sketch. Sometimes there was a dance afterwards, and the audience would file out, and pay to come in again. They would dance until maybe five in the morning.

This was all in the days before Equity insisted that managers had enough money to stage a play. Often if the money did not come in, the manager would disappear, and you would have to try and find another company. Also if you had a disagreement with the manager, you would be fired, just there by the roadside, and you would have to find your own way home from there. Once four or five of us were stranded when the company split up, so we decided to stay on and do a one act play every night. That was very hard work. One night I was allowed to take the money on the door, and some boys outside thought it would be very funny to throw an egg at me. So I was left with a dead chicken sitting on top of my head!

The young Isolde Cazelet

If there was no hall, and we were playing in the middle of the nowhere, we would set up an enormous tent in a field. Our patrons would arrive from the four roads, from all around, walking, on bicycles and in motor cars. One night there were only a few people in the audience, and at the interval they disappeared. We thought that was it, but they came back with a big bunch of flowers for us. Mostly though, we got plenty of people in. It wasn't red carpet treatment exactly, but they were just simply very friendly to us all. Another time, some young lads who had nothing else to do, amused themselves by making numerous holes in our tent. They thought it would be a great idea to slash the tent, and we were supposed to repair it the following day. At this place, I was staying in a converted ambulance in the middle of a bog. There was an actress in this tenting company who used to bring contraband over the border from the Free State to Northern Ireland where there was rationing. It was just after the war, and she would smuggle bags of sugar across. She would keep the border guard chatting while her friend took it over.

I had come over to England a number of times to try to get a footing over here. In the 1950s I'd got a job at Bertram Mills Circus as an usherette around Christmas time, but I didn't get paid till the end of the week, so that meant I had nowhere to stay. I slept every night in a different railway station for a week. The seats were rather hard, but one

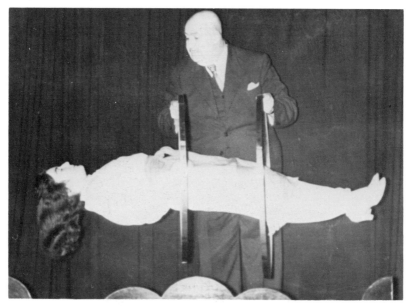

Isolde performing in Bertram Mills Circus.

46

kind porter at Euston allowed me to sit in his chair in his dining room for the night while his wife kept him awake all night in another room, abusing him for doing so. Then when I got paid at the end of the week, I thought that would be fine, but it was late when I got out of the show, and no landlady would take me in, although I had the money. There was great difficulty getting digs, but in the end sombody helped me to find a nice digs.

It was very interesting working in the circus. I was allowed to play with the animals, all the chimpanzees. There was one occasion when I was showing people to their seats, and this lady found she was sitting beside a coloured gentleman, and she insisted on having her seat changed. She wasn't allowed to do so and she had to stay where she was. This was in the 50s when people had notices in shop windows saying, 'No Irish and No Blacks.'

But then in the mid-sixties I came to stay, because I felt there was more opportunity over here. I got a job at the Citizens Theatre in Glasgow playing in 'The Plough and the Stars.' Then I was with a small company touring to schools, doing shows like 'Hansel and Gretel' and 'Snow White'. It was rather tiring because we'd do a show in one place and then have to travel a hundred miles the same day, staying with friends of the man who ran the company. I toured with a company up in Scotland for a while, but I was expected to have a broad Scottish accent which I couldn't do, so that didn't last very long. I've remained in England ever since, except for an occasional holiday in Ireland. The people who come to the theatre are as enthusiastic as ever. There's always an audience for a good play and I hope it will continue like that.

Isolde reading shortly before her death in 1989. She is sadly missed by her family and friends.

JIM COSGRAVE

I was born in 1918, and left school at fifteen. I worked for a year for my uncle, in the grocery business, but he was the meanest man I ever met. I got no wages from him. It's what they call an apprenticeship. You serve three years for nothing. I had a sister over here in England. My brother in law wrote to me, 'Why don't you come over? There's no trouble finding work here.' So I thought, 'Well, I'll have a go. I certainly won't find anything here.' I came over in the early 30s.

I was supposed to be met at Euston Station, but there was nobody there. I asked a fellow how I could get to Victoria Station, and he told me to take a tube. The only tube I'd heard of up till then was a tube of toothpaste, and I couldn't imagine what it would be like! As I got down the platform, I could see the lights of the tube train going away in the distance, so I thought, 'Oh bloody hell, I've missed it.' I thought the next one , like in Ireland, won't be along for another three or four days, but this fellow says to me, 'There'll be one along in a couple of minutes.' So I thought, 'My God, what a place this is! A train every two minutes!'

I was just seventeen, and I could have stayed with my sister, but I didn't want to impose. I wanted a living in job so I could be independent. I took a job at the Windsor Castle, Victoria Station, where I worked very long hours, sometimes up to one o'clock in the morning before I got to bed. And I couldn't sleep because of the noise of the bloody trams running on the tram lines and the overhead wires. The clatter of it was something wicked. I used to write home every night, and my poor mother worried herself sick. I didn't get a bit of sleep for the first three or four weeks.

At first my job was taking the dirty dishes away, but after about six months, I got on the oyster bar and that was great. You were in direct contact with the customers, and we had some real characters there on Victoria Station. The oyster bar men wore white hats, and we used to go through barrels and barrels of oysters a day. You'd think nothing of an order from one of the tables for three or four dozen oysters. We were opening them all day, and it's a tricky job unless you know what you're doing. We also dealt with crabs and lobsters, we carved ham, beef and tongue. We were getting about a pound a week, and a share of what was called 'the trunk'. All the tips were trunked and then shared out, so we'd get an extra pound from that. Two pounds a week was good money in those days.

I was at the oyster bar a couple of years, and then I thought to myself, 'I'll get a job in a place where I can keep my own tips.' I worked then as a waiter in lots of different places. If we were looking for a job we would go round to what we called Starvation Corner. Well, Starvation Corner, any old hot potato will tell you was on the corner of Old Compton Street. We used to stand around there. Every day that we weren't working, we'd sign on first in the morning at the Labour Exchange, and then go straight down to Old Compton Street. The actual official job centre for the catering trade then was Denmark Street, but they never had any jobs there, so it was pointless going there.

That was before the war. When war broke out, I got called up like everyone else. I had to go to Chelsea Barracks to get my uniform. I did four years in the army, and I was discharged in 1944. When they discharged me, they gave me two shirts with no collars, a blue tie and two pairs of army boots. I never did like army boots, so I sold them to a decent old porter in the Grosvenor House Hotel. In the end, he was fined five pounds for being in possession of army property, because the police wouldn't believe that they were my boots to do what I wanted with.

I remember a funny incident at that hotel while I was working there. My job was to keep two big urns supplied for making the coffee. One of the girls spilt a cup of coffee, and a little English fellow-I forget his name-was the manager at the time. And this little Irish fellow who worked there, was given the mop to wipe up the coffee. Well, he was taking it nice and slow like, you know, and this manager, this young, little English man must have seen him through the window in his office door. So he come out to show this Paddy how to clean the floor. He said, 'You don't get a mop like that. I'll show you how to mop. Get hold of this

mop.' The little Paddy said, 'Ah, every man to his own trade.' Well you've never seen a man turn so quick in all your life as that manager. He threw this mop on the floor. He says, 'Come into my office, you're fired!' The Irish man says, 'Yes, and don't forget the two weeks wages I'm owed.' I thought that was really good, first time you ever heard a manager being spoken to like that. And it took an Irishman to do it too.

I remember another Irish fellow , Sugar, we called him, and he was always drinking. He had a dog, a French poodle, a big black one, very tall. That dog would drink as much as his owner. He'd lick the glass tables in the Public Bar. He used to get up and lick all round the table, every table he saw. He really done the bar people a favour there, keeping it clean. God help you if you went to the toilet and the dog saw your pint of mild there!

I used to stand out on my balcony to hear Sugar sing. He had a wonderful voice. One night he was singing away to himself and the dog. And the dog was crying and Sugar was singing away. Next day, I went in to see someone in the pub, and they said, 'Did you hear what happened to Sugar the other night?' Well, in the Evening News it was: 'Dog fined a half crown for being drunk and disorderly'. The magistrate fined the dog! He'd said to the clerk of the court, 'Do you mean to say that the dog was drunk?' The clerk said, 'Ah well, he was barking. The other was singing and the dog was barking.' So the judge said, 'Fine them a half crown each.' And that's a fact.

MAIRA CURRAN

I came from Waterford City. In 1929, when I was two years old, my elder sister and I were put into a home in Clonakilty, where I remained until I was eighteen. We had another sister as well but she was too young to go to this home, she was only ten months old, so she went to foster parents until she was three. Then she went into a home in Kinsale that was similar to where we were and she stayed there.

We went there in March 1929, our father was still alive, but he died in July. I don't know the story, what happened, but we were taken off our mother, we were put into the home and my father was ill in hospital with cancer. Before he died he got all his money together and gave it to the nuns to educate us and bring us up. Most of the children in the home went in there through the Inspector of Cruelty.

The Inspector of Cruelty was the man who went round to all the courts in Ireland on certain days and he came to this particular town where I was once a month. Now his job it was the same as the NSPCC, you know to find out about people who were being ill-treated to bring them before the court. The court said which home they went to, and once you went in there, there was no way you could come out. They made sure you didn't and if a parent came along afterwards, asking that they might be able to have you back (they might say, 'I have a home now and I can give the children a good home'), they wouldn't let them go back until they were sixteen. Then at sixteen most of the children went into service.

The nuns got them jobs, usually in rich people's houses in Ireland and they were just one of many other servants, usually at a very low bottom rung of the hierarchy, as it were. There were very few of us in the home who didn't go into service. My sister and I were two such, and there were another two girls who were in similar circumstances who went out to the national school and were educated.

It was very very bad. We girls who went to the national school were called pets and exceptions and I was being perpetually beaten by other children who were very jealous and really hated me because of it. And even the mistresses who were in charge of us, these were women who had been brought up in the home and they kept them there and they were very bitter women. They were not allowed to go out into the world, they may have been a little bit mentally handicapped, or had some kind of a physical handicap or perhaps they might even have refused to go out when the time came for them to go. So a lot of them weren't fit people to be in charge of us.

We were educated and we were treated differently. We were the nuns' pets. The convent, the home and the school were all one building with doors in between each one. We went to school with the children of the town, and then came back in the evening to the home, through a door and gradually over the years we got to know the children of the town and made a lot of friends that way. We still didn't know very much about the town. We were never allowed to go out on our own. We always went out in a crocodile when we went out anywhere but as we got older and I was about fourteen years of age, they used to send me down to the town for messages. I'd go down to the bank to bring back money, and when I think back on it now, I feel quite awesome about it to see the bank manager counting the money out into the bag, and I had to carry that bag up the town. It never occurred to me that it was something dangerous. You were very safe. The people of the town knew we were from the convent and they wouldn't have done anything to you.

I was very very shy, and I used to blush to the roots of my hair if somebody looked at me even. The first message I ever had to do, I had to go down to the Monseigneur's house with a letter. Now two of the women that worked in the Monseigneur's house had been children in the convent, and that was the work that they got when they left, so I was made very welcome. One of the women came out and said, 'Hello, what's your name?', and told me she had been a child at the convent when she was small. I went into the parlour and then the Monseigner came in and I nearly collapsed on the floor with fear. I never stood next to the Monseigner in my life, let alone mind talk to him, a man towering down on me. I was terrified of him, but he was a wonderful gentleman really, a really nice gentleman.

I always felt that everybody in the town felt so sorry for us. Now I'll tell you something funny that used to happen when we went out. We used to have to walk down to confession every Saturday through the town and back. As we would be walking along in a crocodile, we could hear people saying, 'The poor creatures, God help us, the poor things', and we could never understand, because most of those people were walking with vermins and they had no shoes on their feet and they were decrepit people. We couldn't understand it. And really it gave me an inferiority complex because I felt that I was inferior even to the lowest of the low in the town.

The uniform was a black dress with a white collar and a white apron over it, and then in the evening you had another black dress made in inferior material and another apron over that. You always wore boots, laced up boots and black stockings. The Sunday dress, you had a winter dress and a summer dress for Sunday. In the summer we wore very bright coloured dresses that were really quite outrageously bright, very bright lilac or very yellow. So you really had very few clothes.

Your dress was never washed. All that happened was that you took off the collar in the spring and washed it after you'd worn it all the winter. It was put away in a box, and the dress was taken up to the attic, hung on a sort of a hook in a cupboard with lots of mothballs and that was brought down the next year. If it didn't fit you the next year you got another one that belonged to somebody else and somebody else got yours and then every now and again, you might be lucky and get a new dress every six or eight years. There were so many mothballs in the wardrobes, you'd faint from the smell. You'd be wearing hand-me-downs from other people all the time. I was lucky because I was bigger than everybody else. My nickname was Enormous, so you can imagine how big I was compared to everybody else. I was very lucky because I was one of the ones who had to have a new dress every time, and new boots as well because the boots set aside for my age group didn't fit me.

The normal diet for the children that I remember from day to day, year to year was that in the morning for breakfast we had a couple of slices of bread that had been put into the oven to get crisp and margarine. Lunch was 'wet bread', which was bread with golden syrup watered down. There was so much water in it that the bread was wet. Sometimes we used to have cocoa without any milk or sugar in it. Then we started to get something called carogeen moss. An old women used to collect the special seaweed off the rocks and she used to sell it by the bag to the nuns. They put it in a huge pot and cooked it with milk. Then it was strained off into jugs and poured out and we had that. But unfortunately, the strainer was always leaking so the carogeen used to get into the cup it looked like hens' legs and we used to call it hens' legs. That was lunch. It tasted terrible, but we got used to it after a while and it's supposed to be quite good for you. In the evening at seven o'clock we had a mug of cocoa, no sugar or anything, then two slices of bread, margarine not butter, and sometimes we had wet bread in the evenings as well.

Wednesdays we'd have a plate of porridge with milk and sugar. On Friday we had pease pudding and potatoes and water. Saturday we had rice with no milk and sugar in it, two slice of bread and butter and milk and nothing else. On Sunday we had boiled potatoes with their skins on and a kind of a stew. We didn't have meat, but it was just the juice of the meat. It was really stock and two slices of dry bread.

I remember I used to be absolutely starving and you know the potatoes we'd take the peels of the potatoes. Well after dinner, they used to go out with these great big wooden trays full of the skins of the potatoes and as they would go by, we would all snatch and by the time the tray would get up to the end there would be nothing left in it, that's what we used to eat.

There was an old nun there called Sister Finbar, and she really liked my sister and me. She used to bring out, wrapped up in a cloth, soda bread, with lashings of butter and jam on it, and she used to make us go in the corner and eat it. So every now and again we got that, but it was only certain children got that, so it was another form of favouritism. We used to go and clean out the nuns' cells. That was where the nuns slept and kept all their clothes. It was hard work, but at the end you got something, an apple or a cake, a few sweets or something. I became a great cleaner, and I worked on that so that everyone found out I was good at cleaning cells, so that was a regular pastime in the evening and I got extra food.

When I became a 'mistress', I had a four poster bed with white lace curtains around it in the dormitory. There were four mistress's beds in the dormitory. There were two dormitories, and eight mistresses, four in each, sixty children in each. The four mistresses were in charge of sixty children at night. In the dining room or the refectory as it was called, there were two long tables and the mistresses sat at the head of the table and somebody came round and served them food which was completely diferent to what the children had. It was more like the kind of thing that we eat here, roast dinner on Sunday, pudding, tea and so on.

Like all the mistresses before me, I took my job very seriously. As I had the daylights beaten out of me by the other mistresses, so did I beat the daylights out of the children. That was something that everybody did, but I don't think I went into it with such fervour as some of them did. It wasn't something that I really wanted to do, but I did it because that was how I'd been brought up. When I look back and think on that now, I think how cruel I had been as a mistress to other children . . . well that's how it goes on from one generation to the next.

That was a full time job, a twenty-four hour a day job, day in day out. You never had any time off to do anything for yourself. It was like a dedication, you were really regarded as a nun, same as being a nun, your whole life was given up. You wouldn't have been allowed to go out, the gates were locked at night and we weren't allowed to go out at night.

The only time you went out during the day was when you went out with the children, and Saturday afternoon for two hours you were allowed to go down to the town and you were given money to buy whatever clothes you wanted. Say you wanted a new pair of shoes, you'd go and ask the nun in charge. Now if she decided you didn't need a new pair of shoes she wouldn't give you the money and then you didn't go out. But if she gave you the money you went out and you got your shoes and brought them back and you took them and showed them to her and if they weren't right you got a slap around the face as if you were just six. You'd have to take them back and the next time she'd send down an older mistress with you to collect the kind of shoes she thought you should have.

I got five shillings a week for that. During the day, when the children were at school, the mistresses went into the machine room and they were mending clothes and making clothes and doing jobs like that. I didn't do that. I went into the national school where I had gone to school, and when the nuns would be ill or they might be away somewhere, I would have to take over a class and teach them. I never had any experience of it but because I had been educated and I had got to a secondary school, and had my leaving certificate, I was regarded as being an educated person. I used to take the little children to teach them their alphabet. I was quite good at it. I quite enjoyed it. I did that for the two years I was there.

All the four of us who went on to be educated all got on well. One of the girls when she actually sat for her leaving certificate, I remember seeing it in the newspaper, she came first in the whole of Ireland. Just because they were in bad circumstances it doesn't mean to say that they were stupid or anything.

We realised that we didn't belong to anybody that we were nobody. In spite of the nuns telling us the world was bad and all the people were evil, you wanted to get out and see for yourself, didn't you? That's human nature, and I wanted to get out. As I got older the nuns began to say to me, 'You'd make a very good nun. Why don't you become a nun?' I panicked. I thought, 'I'll never be able to get away. They'll make a nun of me.' I actually ran away once, but when I got out of the convent into the road, I suddenly realised I hadn't got any money and I didn't know what to do, so I went back in again.

But our lives were very sheltered. When I was twenty, I left and I went into nursing. Now we were never told the facts of life. As a matter of fact, it would be true of me to say that I had hardly spoken to a man apart from the monseiguer or a priest or something like that. We were so innocent you see, it never occured to me that men where different to women. When I was due to leave, the head sister called me in one day and said to me, 'Come along we've got to read a book.' I was taken into a room and was sat down on one side of the table and she sat on the other with her rosary in her hands, and she said to me, 'Read that book'. I read it from cover to cover and sat there in front of her reading this book and she never explained anything to me, but I read that book from cover to cover. Well it was the facts of life but it didn't mean a thing to me. I can't remember anything about it, I just remember reading it.

I was never able to voice the opinion that I wanted to go. The day came when I was called into the parlour and told that I was going to England. But first of all an inspector from the Labour Exchange in England came to our town to the hotel. This was a common thing in those days. Anybody who wanted to go nursing or to work in hospitals as a domestic or to work in a factory in England, would be interviewed in the hotel when this person came. So I went to the hotel to be interviewed. I'd rehearsed with the nuns every question that could possibly have an answer to it. I said exactly what I was supposed to say and then in due course, the date for the going came, which was the 7th March 1947.

Maira Curran (left) wtih a friend in Youghal, 1946.

Well on the 7th March 1947 it was a very very bad winter and the snow was feet up outside the door. You couldn't even get outside the door, never mind get to England, so it was postponed for a month. I began to think, 'Will I ever get out of here?' They sent my ticket. It was seven and six from door to door. Everything I went on, I showed my ticket and I got free, seven and six. It took me three days to get to Cardiff and it was the most gruesome experience. I left Clonakilty in the evening and went to Cork and was met by two girls that had been at the convent with me, and the following morning the girls took me to the bus station in Cork for the journey to Dublin. The bus stopped at every little village and every little town. We started off in the morning at eight thirty and we arrived at Dublin at nine thirty in the evening.

That was thirteen hours on this bus and it was freezing cold. They'd be stopping, they'd be getting off and going in the pub. Talk about an outing! I was frozen solid. There was a coach there to take us to the Fitzwilliam Hotel and when we got there there were hundreds and hundreds of people. We all went into this huge hall and we were given cups of tea and sandwiches. Then it came out over the loudspeaker that we were all going to have a medical, so in this huge hall they put up screens the whole way round, and you went behind one screen and got stark naked and they were only screens and you could see everything behind them. You went in and they made you raise up you arms, they looked under both arms and they looked in you hair and they looked in your private parts, and if anybody had vermin they were sent to the baths. Well much to my surprise I was sent to the baths. I must have picked it up travelling during the day and it got on to me. I probably had it in my hair or something. You had to go to the baths and have a bath. Then there weren't enough beds, it was a case of first come, first served. Well of course me being a little bit naïve and slow, by the time I got to bed there was no bed anywhere. They were all crowded in two in a bed, but one women felt sorry for me. She said, 'Squeeze in with us.' It was a single bed and there were two in already, and it wasn't even near a wall, so in the night I just fell out on the floor. I slept on the floor and I was freezing cold.

In the morning we had to walk from the hotel to the boat carrying our suitcases and it was a hell of a long way. Then we got on the boat and I'd never been on a boat in my life so you can imagine! Talk about being sea sick! I was ill and it was the most terrible journey. Then when we arrived at Holyhead, we were shepherded on to a train and before we got on the train we were told we were to get off at Crewe, so we had to get off at Crewe.

It took all day to get up to Crewe, same old thing stopping everywhere. I think we were in one station for about four of five hours. I think there was about thirty of us by the time we got to Crewe. We were met and we were taken to a nice house and given a bed for the night. The next morning, men came with special kind of sashes on them and badges. We had to wear a badge on us as well, but I can't remember what it was like. I was put on the train to Cardiff, and I was told when I arrived at Cardiff there would be somebody to meet me off the train. Well I couldn't see anybody there. I had never gone up and spoken to a person in my life so the first thing I did was sit down on the floor and began to cry because that's what I'd always done, you know, and then it dawned on me that I was out in the world and I was on my own.

But somewhere along the line someone had told me not to talk to a man, but you could always talk to a woman. So I went and asked a woman where St Winifred's Hospital was and she put me on a bus and told me where to get off. It was a hell of a long walk and I had these two big suitcases. When I arrived at the hospital, I'll tell you this much, after three days travelling, I was completely exhausted.

They were very pleased to see me at the hospital. I met the night sister who had been brought up in the same home as me, so that was a good friend for me. Then there was also a nurse there from Clonakilty, who was a trained nurse, and she was working there as well, so I had the two of them. When I got there I had two or three days off to rest after the journey. I went down to the night sister's house. We sat down and we began to talk about the convent and she told me a lot of things.

It was a private hospital run by nuns, so it was really home from home. They were really good to me and really tried to make me feel at home and to help me as much as they could.

The first day I was on the ward, the sister said to me, 'Come along, Nurse O'Rourke, and help me with this patient.' It was a men's ward and Mr Jones was his name. I went in and she was taking his stitches out and she pulled the bedclothes back and he was uncovered and I suddenly saw his private parts. Well, I never knew that men and women were different, and I let out a scream. She put her hand across and slapped me round the face and said, 'Control yourself, Nurse O'Rourke.' She didn't know why I was screaming, and I never told her, but I shall never forget that though, when I saw that, oh my God, you know.

I had a hell of a life then with the men on the ward. They soon discovered how shy I was, and they used to tease me like mad. Their greatest moment was when they wanted a bedpan. They'd say to me, 'Nurse can you get a bedpan?' And then everyone would say, 'Oh, I want one as well', and I'd have to come in with six bedpans piled one on top of the other. And then I'd have to go round and give them the bedpans and I'd pull the curtains around and when they'd get me in behind the curtains they'd start squeezing me. My face used to be so red. I really dreaded going in there. They used to torment the life out of me, and everything I'd say they would take the mickey and make fun of it. But it was good in the long run, you had to snap out of it, otherwise you were just miserable. I soon lost my shyness.

I went out with the other nurses, but not with men or to dances, nothing like that. As a matter of fact I couldn't understand what anybody was saying, although it was English. Don't forget that I'd never been outside the convent in eighteen years, so all I'd heard was the people around me talking in the same accent. It took me ages to understand. We all went out together, all the nurses. We used to walk along with our arms around one another, down the road, singing and shouting. We used to go to the pictures and you know, I really didn't understand anything that was being said. They must have thought that I was quite stupid because when I'd come out I'd say, 'What was that about?'

I stayed there a year and the reason that I went there was because it was my first step into the world. Going to the nuns in that hospital was like the breaking in, getting used to the world. You only stayed there a year, and then you were expected to leave and go on and do your general training. When I was there about nine months, the matron sent for me and she said, 'It's time you were applying to go to the General Hospital.' She gave me a lot of help, the addresses, names of hospitals in London, and told me to think over which one I would like to go to. I picked the Royal Northern Hospital, I don't know why. Maybe somebody told me it was a good one. That was the one I picked in London in Holloway Road.

I was very, very, very unhappy. The sister was really nasty to me, so much so that one day I thought of doing myself in. I really didn't know how I was going to do it, but I thought that I had to. There were gas fires like boxes and all along the bottom inside there were all these gas jets, and I was going to blow them out and gas myself. But somebody came in and caught me out before I had a chance, and I got into trouble for being where I wasn't supposed to be. So that put paid to that.

I was called to see the matron, and I was absolutely terrified. But she was so lovely, so nice, compared to the sister. She was a human being and she said to me, 'Now Nurse O'Rourke, I'm very sorry to have to tell you that you won't be doing your general nursing training because we don't think that you're stable enough.' Well I was crying a lot of the time. Then she went on to say, 'Well you would make a very good nurse, you did very well but you're not quite right, not quite balanced.' I started bawling my eyes out then, and I said, 'You can't do that to me, I have nowhere to go.' And she said, 'Oh come here, don't cry like that, we won't send you away', she said. We've got another hospital in Southgate, and it's called a hospital of recovery where our patients go after they've had their operations. We'll send you out there.'

So I was more or less turfed out. That day the ambulance was taking the patients and I was put in the ambulance and taken there. Up till then I did cry a lot. I can remember being torn with grief with the way I were being treated. The rest of the girls were unhappy too, but they were more adjusted to the world and they could cope with it. They knew that it was temporary, but to me that was the end of the world. So I went and there were two wards there, male and female, and I must say I quite enjoyed it. It was a very small place compared to the Royal Northern and it was called Grovelands Park, a very old house and during the war it was used for war casualties, and there were a lot of them there and other patients as well.

I fitted in lovely. The matron took a liking for me. I went there as a probationer nurse, and I stopped there for two years. I got a lot of nursing experience there, I was in charge of the ward, doing things I would never have done in the other place. I proved to be quite smart, and the matron realised that, and I soon got myself into a position there where I was in charge of things. I always got on very well there.

Around this time, when I was about twenty-two, all the rest of the girls were going out with boys, it was all boys, you know, so I started going out to dance halls with Irish girls, meeting Irish men and going to dances then.

I was beginning to get very naughty, to rebel, and the matron was very strict. When you stay out the night, you have to sign a book to say that you are not coming back, but the following evening you have to be in before ten. I never signed the book, and then I never came back at ten, and I was out for two whole days, and when I came back the matron was ever so worried. She said, 'Where have you been?' and of course I wouldn't tell her. She said, 'You know that I could dismiss you here and now, but I'm not going to. But if you do it again, you are out.' So the very next weekend I did it again. I don't know why I did it but I was throwing everything to the wind, really rebelling. So she did, and I left.

And do you know that that matron gave me a marvellous reference. She really was quite nice. I think she knew what I was going through although I never really said much to her. I never regretted it, that was it, I was out and free.

I found myself a living-in job looking after children, and it was very easy for me to get into that as a nanny, because I had the little bit of nursing experience. Well I started off with English people. I worked with a banking family, bankers, in a great big beautiful house in Hertfordshire. I stayed there for two years, and I had my own room, but I was treated like a servant there. I wasn't allowed to go in with the family or anything. I sat alone in the kitchen in the evening and waited on table.

They used to go out hunting, they had their own horses and that. One morning the woman had her horse ready to go when the telephone rang. She had to go to the telephone, so she said to me, 'Hold the horse for a minute'. Well of course the horse could tell I didn't know what I was doing. It went up on its front legs like that and I ran. I thought I'd better get out of the way quick, and it rushed out on to the road. When the woman came out and said, 'Where's the horse?', I said, 'It's run away.' She got in her jeep and rushed off. The horse was galloping along the road, and she stopped it and led it back. She was furious with me, but I wasn't used to horses, well I was terrified of them.

Then I saw in the paper that somebody was looking for a nanny down in Hove. I thought that that would be a nice place to go, near the sea, so I applied for it and I got it. It was £4 a week there, with a very nice Jewish family, and I was one of the family. I fould the Jewish people wonderful to work for, really nice people. There was none of that servant treatment. When I left there I still stayed with Jewish families, back in London.

I went back to London and I worked for a Jewish family where there were two children, and I was getting £4 a week there. I was with them for about 3 years, because I really really liked it there. I was one of the family. I had my meals with them, except on Friday evenings, because that is their Sabbath, and it is special, you know, they light candles and they have special food, that was their special evening. The older child stayed up for that as well.

Maira at the Royal Northern Hospital Recovery Unit at Southgate, 1948.

Every summer, we used to go down to Westgate on Sea, and stay in a hotel with other relatives of the family who all had their own nannies. Every year we'd all be there, and they let us go out in the evening, and looked after the children for us. Then at the weekend all the relatives would come down and you had those two days off. There was one uncle there, he was really really fond of the children, and he took us out in a paddleboat. I remember him doing the paddling, and I've got the little fellow, the boy of two or three, on my lap, and we are going all around in the sea. It was very very good.

They were Jews who had come from Europe just before the war, like displaced persons who had nothing, and they were getting their lives together. During the war they used to make army uniforms, but now they had got round to making ordinary clothes for people. They had clothes factories, all this lot. They used to play poker, they used to go to a different house each night to play, and when it was to my house, where I was, I had the day off. Then I'd come back late, and they'd all be in the sitting room playing poker. One night, one of the husbands said to me, 'Well I think it is about time you had some nice clothes. Would you like to come to my factory tomorrow, and you can have everything at cost price.' So I went to this great big shed where there were all these clothes laid out, you know, jumpers, skirts, oh fabulous stuff there was, and I picked what I wanted and then he told me how much it was, and the whole thing came to just a few pounds, I think £6, and I had everything, I had shoes, a coat, a dress, a cardigan, underwear, I had the lot. And he said to me, 'You needn't give it back to me at once, just ten shillings a week. I remember that because I thought that it was marvellous, that really was marvellous.

Another thing too, when the children used to get invited to parties. I used to go with them and come back in a taxi. They used to have people coming all dressed up, clowns and all that, it was really good. You know it was a wonderful life, I'd never experienced anything like it in my life.

My youngest sister came from Ireland around about this time. She had been working in Ireland and she wanted to come over to be near me. I took the day off to help her find a job. She had interviews for three different jobs, but when we got there, either the jobs were not there, or they were not looking for somebody like her. She was looking for a job in a hotel, because that was the type of work that she had done in Ireland.

At the end of the day there was no job, so I telephoned the house where

I was working, and the woman said, 'Oh bring her back here, I'm sure somebody in my family will have her, if she's anything like you.' So I took her back to my Jewish family, and they telephoned their sister, and she said, 'Yes definitely, we'll have her.' So she was working with this woman's sister. I was in Stamford Hill, and she was living in Maida Vale, really not far away. We had the same day off, we always went out together, and you see gradually I was beginning to get a little bit of a life together.

Right beside where I had been working in Hove, with the previous family, there was a children's home. When I had any time off, I used to go down there. That was the kind of life that I was used to, and there were nuns there and it was comforting. That's where I met my husband actually. He was a widower, and when his wife died, he put his four children into this home in Hove. He used to come down and see the children, and one of the nuns introduced me to him.

I used to take the children out to the beach, all the children, anybody, and he used to take his children out to the beach and I used to see him. He was looking for somebody to look after the children, and I thought, well I'm doing that now, aren't I? I hadn't really thought that much about it, but of course the children I was looking after were not my responsibility to feed and clothe. I didn't realise the extent of what I was taking on, when I took them on. The youngest child was five and the eldest was nine.

One of the welfare workers said to me, 'It never works out when a woman marries and takes on a man's children.' But I have never been one to take advice from anybody, never, because I'm pigheaded. I continued to see him when I came to London, and I never took her advice, and she was right. You see, when a man's wife dies, the man becomes very possessive of the children, because he is the mother and the father, and even though he might take on another woman, he's only taking on that woman really, to look after the children, but not to be a mother. It's very difficult to have to live with that because you see, all the time you have to listen to what a wonderful woman she was, and what she did and all the rest of it. The first love is the only love. To a man, no other woman will match up to that and I defy any woman who argues with that, and other people have told me that same thing.

He had a prefab. When his wife died, they had a flat, but he didn't want to stay there when the children went away so the council gave him a prefab. So when we got married, I moved into the prefab in

Bolingbroke Grove in Wandsworth. There were four children in his first family, and then I had one girl, and then we had four more children after. So there were nine altogether.

I discovered jumble sales, not long after I was married and they turned out to be the most wonderful thing. We used to get the Wandsworth Borough News and in there it showed you all the places where they had the jumble sales. We'd go from one to another, as things were very cheap. Sometimes on a Saturday we'd go to three or four of them. We knew what we wanted and always picked nice things. Getting on the committees in my children's schools, and being in charge of a jumble sale or something like that, I had the pick of the best. There were eight children then, and he couldn't afford to clothe that many.

My eldest daughter, she went away to school. In the early days of the marriage, things weren't working out and she was getting the rough end of it, and I thought it best to get her out. The Catholic Childrens Society gave her a very good education, so I was very pleased about that. They were very good to her, they sent her to a private boarding school down near Bexhill, she had a marvellous education, all the O levels and A levels and went on to become an occupational therapist. I didn't have to pay anything but I promised myself that if I am ever in a position to give it back, then I would.

When I left Ireland first of all, I used to go back to the convent. When you come to England for 7/6d you were allowed to go back every year for a holiday for the 7/6d. When you went back to the convent, they treated you like a lady and you had special food and you were a VIP really. However you weren't allowed to go out in the evening, and I had to stay at the convent as I couldn't have afforded a holiday. It was very narrow, but I liked it. They were very proud of me and I remember one of the nuns saying to me, 'Would you stop using all those big words, we don't understand all those big words here.' It was a simple sort of language that they speak, and being in England, I was using all the big words that they use in England, they use longer words in England. I remember different nuns would come forward and I would have to sit down and relate the whole episode from when I arrived there, all the ins and outs, and all the questions about everything. I think the verdict when I was leaving was that they were quite pleased with me. I managed to go back on holiday for the first two years and then, when I wasn't doing so well here, well I couldn't go back, could I?

I went back there last year for the first time ever since those first two years when I visited. I went back with my sister. Things haven't changed at all, exactly the same. I learned a lot of nice things about the nuns. They were all there together since they were young, all women, and they were so happy, and genuinely happy. They were nice and friendly, and making allowances for one another, saying the best about one another. I felt that if all the people in the world were like that, my goodness me, what a wonderful world it would be. I had never really seen them all together like that as women, you know, it was so nice. They were so proud of me and you could see how fond of us they were and it was genuine. When I was a child there I never really felt that they liked me but I'm sure they did. One of them said to me, 'Oh I remember you, you had a lot of brains but you were a little monkey.' That's the kind of thing they would say to you when you were a little child, and they were still saying it. Now she taught me when she was only a bit of a girl, just sixteen, just entered, and I was about twelve, and she was five years older than me. Yet she still thinks of me as a little monkey.

Now when I was a child, I could almost say that I hated the nuns. I knew that I was there and that that wasn't normal. I'd see children from the town coming in each day, who had homes and parents, and I hadn't. Now the nearest people to blame were the nuns, and I blamed them. When I left the convent and met my mother before she died, I didn't really blame her because I'd almost got over it. Then as the years went by and I went through all my difficult times, I began to realise how secure we were there, we were fed and clothed and looked after, even though we were a big crowd, there were over a hundred of us. We did mean something to them.

MARY GALVIN

I was born in 1915. I come from Waterford City. I went to school to the 'Sisters of Mercy', in Philip Street in Waterford and also to the 'Sisters of Charity', Parnell Street, Waterford.

The earliest memory I have is when the priest of St. John's Church and the Mayor of Waterford, Mayor Jones, gave an excursion to Tramore for the poor of the city. We started from the courthouse grounds and we were given a bag of 'goodies', as it's called now. There was an apple, an orange, sweets, a sandwich and some cakes. And we went up to Tramore and we had a marvellous day on the games. That was the earliest I remember. That was our first visit to the seaside. Most of us was bare-footed because we hadn't any shoes in those times. Times were ever so hard.

I remember my mother used to give me a penny to go down to the square, which was a market place, for a pen'orth of cauliflower leaves, because times were very, very hard. My mother had three of us in family, there were two brothers and myself. My father served in the First World War, he was given a pension of fifteen shillings and sixpence a week. A shilling of that was for me because I was born during the war, but there was nothing for my brothers.

I never remember getting anything new, never, until I started to work in a bag factory and I worked for seven shillings a week, and I was given a shilling out of that for pocket-money. A shilling was a lot of money in those times because you could do a lot with a shilling. You could go to the pictures in the night-time for tuppence, and fish and chips was fourpence, and you'd get a scallop, which was done with a large potato, and you'd get it sliced dipped in batter for a happenny. They were very hard times but they were happy times and you always remember and talk about the times.

Pancake night, a couple of us would get together, in or about the same age then, and we'd go around to the people that was rich . . . well they were rich in comparision to us . . . and we'd sing outside their door,

'Old Jack Larkins, silk and satin,
Give the poor man something,
A bit of bread, a roasted egg,
A pancake or a dumpling.'

So we came to a doctor's house, she was a lady doctor, and my friend told us all to go behind the corner and he'd share with us what he'd get. So we did as we were asked, a few minutes went by and he came behind the corner and he was saturated from his head to his toes. The doctor was after throwing a basin of water up over him. That's really the truth.

And when we'd go to confession on Good Friday, there was always a shopkeeper there, very good living woman, and generous, and if we were sitting waiting to go into the confessional and if she was sitting alongside of us, we'd let her go first and she always gave us sixpence. And we just let her go first for the sake of getting the sixpence. Well, the sixpence wasn't left to us, it was taken from us by our parents, and we were given tuppence.

I started work in 1933 when I was fifteen. We left school at an early age then. I went to work in a bag factory. It was a British firm, now no longer in existence. It was very hard work and dirty work. We got sacks in that had been used for animal feed and flour and they had a blowing machine. You'd have to put two bags on the machine and turn them inside out. Sometimes if they were heavy sacks, your hands would hit up at the machine and you'd have very sore knuckles.

We weren't making the bags then, we were getting them in from farmers and that and sending them out, mending them, darning them on the machine. I did the cleaning of them for a bit and after that I was put on a machine, darning them. I was paid seven shillings a week, and I worked from nine in the morning to six at night, including Saturday morning. There was no such thing as holidays in those times.

We used to go to the dance very often. It was in a small hall in New

Street. And if we hadn't the fourpence to get in we'd ask the chap on the door to let us in on credit, which he never got paid. It was a great time. But I wasn't very successful in the dance because I was very heavy on my feet, which I still am, it was like bringing a carthorse around the floor. There might be some particular lad that you'd put you eye on, and he'd never ask you to dance, he'd go off with somebody else. But I did meet my husband at a dance. We always walked home after the dance because we weren't living far away. Waterford City was not very big, everybody knew one another.

Oh there was a lot of difference when I came to London for the first time. It was a terrible change. The first time I came, I only stayed three months. I had left the children to my mother in Ireland, because my husband was already over here, he'd come over first during the war. We were married in 1936, and had our children in Ireland, then he came over again into the building trade, because there was nothing doing in Ireland, and I came over after him.

There were no opportunities in Ireland at all. A man had five children. At Christmas time he'd get 4 days work, what was called the 'Grant' and no matter how the weather would be, he still had to stay out under it digging roads and unless a man had five children he wouldn't get that. My husband was on the dole. There was no work in Ireland. I had five children before I went to work. We had eighteen shillings and sixpence a week to keep seven of us.

The labour exchange would send a man out to different farmers. If he went to a good farmer, he'd get his food for the day, but no money and some were unlucky. Some of the farmers they'd go to wouldn't even make them a meal. We would go out picking blackberries to sell. Oh it was a terrible hard time. The husbands left the country to come over here, and the wives and children followed them on. They never went back because there was nothing to go back to.

I travelled by boat and train, yes I remember it well. We were standing in the boat, cos there was no place to sit down. It was a cattle boat actually and it was £5 to come over here then. And the sea-sickness was terrible. You were coming over and you didn't know where you were coming to.

I was very very lonesome, especially as the children were in Ireland. I worked early mornings, and no matter who you'd meet at that time of the morning, they'd never say good morning to you. I was doing cleaning in Selfridges of Oxford Street and at that time it was a half-crown an hour. And the work was hard because winter and summer, even when the snow would be on the steps, you'd have to go out and scrub the steps down.

I remember the job in Selfridges. Half-past six in the morning I had to be in Oxford Street. There was one very cold morning in the winter and the foreman gave off to me because I wouldn't take the snow off the step, so I got me bucket of dirty water and I let him have it, I got so fed up. So that finished me job in Selfridges to tell you the truth. He had the bucket of dirty water over his face.

It was very, very hard. But I got very lonesome and homesick with the children away from me in Ireland, and after three months I got fed up and went home. It was nice going home to Ireland, but then I got the urge to come back to London. The bit of money I had was gone, so I borrowed the fare from me uncle and came back. I brought my family over the second time I came. After that, I never went home again except for holidays.

When I came back, I got three cleaning jobs. I used to go to one job at half-past six to eight o'clock in the morning, come home, have a cup of tea, and at nine o'clock I'd go and I'd clean out a pub. At two o'clock I'd go to a shop in Bayswater and I'd clean that up and at 3 o'clock I went down to a cafe at Westminster Hospital and I worked there until 8 o'clock. I went from work to bed. I'd be so tired I wouldn't want to do anything else, after slaving all day.

There was nothing easy about cleaning work at that time because there was no mops, everything was done on your knees with a scrubbing brush. It was very hard work in them times, and each job paid out the same amount of money at half-a-crown an hour. The same work today, some jobs pay £3 an hour, which is a great change.

I found the people over here were very different from the Irish people, much different. Nobody would bid you the time of the morning. It was a terrible change for anybody emigrating over here. I mean if Ireland was then as it is today there'd be none of this in this country. None of us at all, that's what brought us over like every other immigrant that's in this country. They all had to leave their own country to get a living. Nobody wanted to leave their own country where their roots were.

Accomodation here, it was a problem. I found out that if you had a dog you'd get in quicker than if you had a child. Once you said you had a child you were left out, they didn't want to know. Well I had one furnished room for my eldest son which I paid four pound a week for and I had my eldest daughter. I had a room and a kitchen and my eldest daughter stayed with me and that was also four pound a week, which was £8 a week. And there was still two of my family in Ireland and I sent home money for them and clothes. Then we got a couple of rooms in Bayswater, so eventually I brought over the rest of my family and from there we settled in.

After that, we saved up what we could. In the end we were able to buy our own house in 1959. That's because I was working, and my husband and then three in me family was working and two going to school.

When we bought our house it was £75 deposit and it was £5.19.6d a month off of the mortgage. But it was a comfortable little house and when we bought it there was an old lady living upstairs, but we managed all right. We modernised it and we had a nice home there. So then the old lady died and I was able to take in one of my daughters over from Ireland that was married, and she had no place, so she had a kitchen and a room upstairs. It was some happy times for me when she came over here.

Every Saturday night we used to go to a pub called The French Horn and Half Moon. There used to be competitions and singing and I used to get up to sing.

> 'You were everywhere,
> Everywhere you're there,
> Night and day I've spent with you,
> Though I know you're gone,
> Your memory lingers on,
> Like a haunting memory.'

I had a good voice in me time, but now I can hardly talk. We used to have a good time. The Babycham was one and sixpence. We went to the Metropolitan every Saturday night. It was a night out at 'The Met' for Music Hall. We used to have Max Miller and we had Jimmy O'Dee from Dublin and his group. One night, Jimmy O'Dee had Irish dancers and Noel Purcell was with him and Maureen Potter. It used to be lovely. We'd be upstairs in the 'gods'. We used to bring the youngest daughter then and she can remember it. This is me home now, just the same as if I was living in Ireland. I have a lot of friends and I know almost everybody in this area of Wandsworth the same as I did in my own city.

There's more of a social life for me now. I joined a club down in York Gardens for the senior citizens. And now I've joined this club, for Irish pensioners. And all my family is over here now. They all have their own homes, except for one daughter lives in Mayo in Ireland. I don't go back to Ireland since I lost me father and mother. I used to go home twice a year, in the summer and at Christmas, but there's nothing in Ireland now to bring me home.

I never felt that I wanted to go back and live in Ireland. No, I never did. Because my family were over here so it would be spliting up the family and I like to have my family. It was a heart break when I had to leave them when I first came over here, it was really hard.

I didn't get a bad deal being in this country but what I got in this country, I worked very hard for, and so did my husband and my family.

The Battersea Irish Elderly Group

JULIA GRIFFIN

My family was very poor. I was the youngest of nine children, six boys and three girls, near a little town called Athlone in Westmeath. My father was eighteen years older than my mother, and she was forty-two when she had me, so he was sixty when I was born. Talk about over-crowding, we had one room and a kitchen and a little yard and we lived there till I was ten.

We slept with two beds in the room. We always slept three or four in each, two in each end, or however many it took to get us all in. There were children in the foot and the head of the beds, and someone had to sleep in the bed with my parents. We had what was called a settle bed which was sort of like a closed in settee, which was a seat in the day and at night you opened it up and the mattress and the clothes were folded in there.

My father was a herdsman for the gentry on a big estate and we lived in the little gate lodge. He worked for a Miss Kilduff, her parents had been there before that. They were great Catholics, this family he worked for, and they had an uncle who was an archbishop. I remember they paid my father sixteen shillings wage, though it might have been less earlier on. But they wouldn't give you a drop of milk to put in your tea. On the other side of us there was an English Protestant lady, a Miss Hagan, and her three sisters. I don't think there was any man there, their brother was an army captain somewhere, and they were the best neighbours we ever had. They really looked after us and helped us. We could always go and knock on their door if we hadn't any milk or anything (and very often we hadn't) and they'd always give us something. Although there was so many of us, we never went hungry.

My father didn't have any land to grow his own food, but we had a tiny little garden. It was not really enough, with all the kids to play in it, but my mother loved flowers, so we had a few flowers in the front, but there wasn't enough to grow anything really except maybe a few heads of cabbage.

My sister was eight years older than me, so she helped my mother a lot. I think my mother must have had a very hard time. We had a great big arch with the open fire, and you had to hang the pots on top of this and boil the water. We had a tap that was outside the door, but at least we had running water. All the water had to be boiled. We didn't have any fancy dining room tables, we had a great big kitchen table which was just scrubbed and scrubbed till it was white.

My mother used to boil all the washing. It was washed first, then it was put into this great pot with washing soda and washing powder, and boiled. And after that there was all the rinsing, then it was blued, with the blue bag, and put out till it got to a certain point of drying and brought in and starched, and out again. Then we had the little hand irons, which you had to heat on the fire. Well of course they got dirty while they were heating, so you'd clean this on a sod of turf and a piece of cloth, and by the time you got it clean, you see half the heat was gone out of it.

I remember the flour came in large sacks made from strong cotton, Irish Purity it was called, and there was a picture on the sack of an Irish colleen with a green dress and a white apron and a red shawl. Over her arm she carried a whicker basket with a sheaf of wheat laying across it. These sacks were very useful. When you unpicked these sacks and boiled them they made pillow cases, or four stitched together made a large sheet for the bed. Mother would make our underwear from them. It took many boilings to remove the picture from the sacks, so I often went to school with 'Irish Purity' across my back or chest.

The boys were very fussy, because my elder brothers were going to dances and things at this time, and their collars would have to be ironed until they shone. My eldest brother was quite good, he'd take a turn at doing his own trousers on the settle bed. It was six feet long, and when it was closed up it was like a long narrow table, and that was marvellous for ironing trousers on. And I can remember my brother Jack used to lay a blanket on top of the settle bed, and sometimes this would be Sunday afternoon, and although we had such a house full of people, others came. I think when you have a large family, a lot of others call, so all my brothers' friends would come in.

They would bring their best clothes, their trousers on Sunday, and my brother would be pressing trousers for a couple of hours doing theirs as well. This was because they would all be going to the dances on Sunday night — Sunday night was the big night for dances in Ireland. They were held in halls, in Athlone which was quite a big town, and we lived about half a mile outside the town, just an easy little walk.

We lived there till I was ten, so you see I was only very small when they were going off to these dances, but I remember looking forward to them going to the dances, everyone getting ready, and girlfriends coming in. That was all very exciting.

I had a very happy childhood in spite of, you know, half the time no milk in your tea, or maybe butter on your bread.

Going to the bog to bring home the turf

My family loved music, and they loved singing. The neighbours all came to our house and they used to play. Our nearest neighbours lived in a railway cottage and they had one room and a kitchen as well. They only had about five kids, and there was all of us, but all the crowd came to our house. Sunday was the day. Everyone went to church in the morning, and then there were football matches in the afternoon. Sunday was the day to enjoy yourself. If there wasn't a dance in the town, we had dances in our house. We had a wind-up gramophone.

Saturday, people would be working. My eldest brother was earning ten shillings a week, and there was a music shop in town and he would buy records. Saturday nights he would bring home a record and that would be played and played until everyone knew it off by heart. We would be sitting up in the bed listening to it. I can remember him bringing home 'Ramona', and the one about the man who broke the bank at Monte Carlo.

There were always people in with accordions and fiddles, and my father used to love to sing. We all joined in — while we were very little, we'd be put in a room, we were supposed to be in bed, but of course we were sitting up listening. There were a lot of the Irish songs. If a neighbour came in you'd say, 'Oh, so-and-so's here, let's hear such-and-such a song'.

My eldest brother used to sing 'Danny Boy', and 'If I had the Wings of a Swallow' — that was one of his favourite ones.

'If I had the wings of a swallow
I'd travel far over the sea,
And the rocky old road I would follow,
To a spot that is heaven to me,
There's someone I'd bless with true tenderness,
And her lips I'd caress when I bring happiness.
That dear little town in the old County Down
It will linger way down in my heart.
Though it never was grand, it is my fairyland,
Just a wonderful world set apart.
Oh my island of dreams, you are with me it seems
Though I care not for fame or renown.
Like the black sheep of old I return to the fold,
Little town in the old County Down.'

Some of Julia's family sitting on the trunk of a tree which had been cut down when electricity came to Athlone in 1930.

My father had some lovely old songs — there was one which I've never been able to see the words of anywhere, which was called 'The Holy Church of Rome', and I'd love someone to have the words of it, because that was one of my earliest childhood memories. He had another one that was 'The Blackbird of Sweet Avondale' — he sang that beautifully, so people would always ask, you know — 'Come on, Tom, give us the Blackbird', and he would sing The Blackbird.

My mother could sing but she never sang, she was very shy, like me, I was very shy. My brother Pat used to find comical songs, so he had one that was called 'The Old Leather Breeches', so that was favourite, you know, for him to be asked to sing. I remember it was about a couple who kept a little hotel or eating-house or whatever, and one very snowy night some very rough people called on them, and the man didn't want to let them in. But his wife said, 'Oh Paddy, you'd better go down there and let them in, because they're breaking in the door.' So he let them in, and they wanted food, and they had no food, because they'd been snowed under for weeks. So he decided that he would cut up his leather breeches and boil them and he gave it to them to eat. While they were eating they thought it was great, and then somebody found a button, and they saw that they'd been eating these old leather breeches.

My youngest brother Peter used to recite:

I am my mother's little man
I'm the chief of all the clan
I know there's Ned and Ted and Fred
But if you please, 'tis I'm the head
I tend the walks, I sweep the floor
I go on errands to the store
And any day I'd walk a mile
To see my pretty mother smile
You needn't laugh because I'm small
Just being big sir isn't all
I'm as good a man as any man
I do everything I can.

Pat Rush, Julia's brother, taking horses to the hunt.

When I was ten, we left that house, because my father got what was called a labourer's cottage, which was about a mile further out of the town and we had three rooms and a kitchen. That was marvellous, but we didn't have any water. We were worse off for water, because we had to walk about a half a mile to the nearest pump.

That was spring water we had there, not town water, but it meant you had to walk in all weathers, and carry buckets of waters in. In the winter we had a great big barrel, like what the beer comes in, or tar barrels, they were, and so, from the eave-chute they would have a pipe, and we could fill up the barrel all the winter, so you got lovely rainwater to wash your hair in, and that was fine. In the summer time there wouldn't be

79

any other water, so you had to carry buckets of water for the washing and everything.

I went to school until I was thirteen when my sister got married. Then there was no-one to help my mother, and we still had five boys at home. I should have gone back to school on 6th September, but my birthday came on the 15th of September, so I never went back to school. I was home then, you know, giving my mother a hand with all the cleaning and washing and cooking and drying. I did that until I was eighteen.

I never had a job. There were not many jobs going. There was a factory in the town, but my mother wouldn't hear of us looking for a job although we had nothing, and we were terribly poor, still you just didn't work in a factory if you were country people as we were. So it seemed natural that I would stay at home and I would help my mother. The only money I ever got in Ireland was a shilling on a Sunday night to go to Irish dances.

I didn't have many boyfriends, because I always went with my brother. He looked after me, we went together. But sometimes he'd have a girl, and I'd have a boy. I had a soldier boyfriend once, and of course he had to get back to the barracks, and we lived a mile and a half out of the town of Athlone, so he'd see me a little bit out of the road, and then my brother would wait for me and take me home.

We went mostly to the ceilidhs in the Gaelic League Hall, and there I did all the Irish dances, Walls of Limerick, Haymakers' Jig, sixteen-hand reels, and the Siege of Ennis, and we loved it.

In the summertime, there would be open air dancing. They had a wooden floor, and perhaps there would be a marquee, but sometimes you had no cover and you could dance until it got dark. When the nights started getting shorter, the halls would open up more, and my younger brother and I, we liked the Irish dances best. Funnily enough all the rest of the the boys, and my sister, they preferred what was called the modern dance, the waltz and the quickstep.

In the summer before I was eighteen, I had a cousin that lived in England. She'd been in England for years, and she came home. She said to me, 'I could get you a job if you came to England', so I thought that was marvellous. I'd have a job and some money of my own. When she went back, she got me a job at a convent in Welling in Kent. She wrote to me and I wrote back to the nuns and it was all arranged. I was to be a sort of general helper, on the domestic side. I had to wait till I was eighteen before I could get a visa to come. I came over on 2nd November 1943.

I've often thought, why didn't I try for the A.T.S., or the Land Army? Or there were other things I maybe could have done and I might have been happier. But then on the other hand, probably my parents wouldn't have allowed me to come over to do something like that. Because I came to the convent, they were not too worried about letting me come, because they felt I would be looked after.

It was a great adventure for me, I'd never been anywhere, I'd never been on a train — only once in my life before that, I went to Galway, and that was the only time I'd ever been on a train — so I'd never been to Dublin even. I thought it was marvellous. I often think now I was stupid, and I shouldn't have come, and what would it have been like if I'd . . . but, anyway, I did come, and you know, I did like it, I enjoyed it.

The first night on the train, before we got into London, the train got held up because there was an air-raid, somewhere along the line. We got in late, but my cousin was there at Euston to meet me, and she took me to her digs for the night. In the morning, she took me to the convent and handed me over to the nuns.

I was a very young 18, and very shy, but I loved it at the convent, and they were very nice to me, very, very good. I was a general helper on the domestic side. I was paid one pound a week, with ninepence docked out of that for insurance.

The raids were quite bad when I first came over, but I used to sleep through them. I'd be upstairs, and they'd say, you know, 'Wasn't it bad last night?' and I didn't know, I hadn't heard them. But after a week a so, they were nervous to leave me upstairs, because they'd be all be getting up, so they used to come and knock me up if there was a bad raid. We didn't have a shelter in the convent, and so we went down into what was called a covered way. It was a wide passage where the school went over — and there were two or three storeys of the school building on top of it, so we used to go down there when the raids were bad, and a lot of other people came in as well. And the nuns were very kind. We prayed all night, the nuns would be saying the rosary, and we all joined in.

There was times I was very homesick. I wrote home a lot, and they wrote back. We were such a big family, always singing and dancing and everything, and I missed them.

I can remember crying often, being homesick, especially when St Patrick's Day came, that was heartbreaking, because it used to be such a day at home, you know. They would march through the streets, and all the boys' bands playing, and the girls, we all wore our first communion dresses and veils. We had a great procession, you know, all round the town, it was really a great day. So it was an awful sad day, to be on your own, you know, in a strange country. But the nuns were good to me and tried to cheer me up.

Through the church I met a few friends, like Kathleen with her bicycle. We used to have bikes, and cycle over the countryside, about twenty miles and take picnics and that was very nice.

I went home for a short period in 1945 when my father was ill. That's the last Christmas I spent in Ireland. I've never been in Ireland for Christmas since. After that I came back and worked in the convent until 1947. I was sweeping and cleaning, peeling buckets full of potatoes, helping to dish up the dinners, clearing tables and so on. I thought I would like to do something else. I thought I might go into nursing, and I sent off a few applications, but because I'd only been to school for such a short time, I wasn't accepted. At this time they were crying out for nurses. I wrote back to one hospital, and said I thought it was so unfair, because if I'd been able to stay on at school I could have done all right because I was quite good at school work. I was quite happy and prepared to learn and to study. They wrote back after that and said they would see me, but I'd been turned down so much, I thought, no I won't do it.

Somebody told me that there was a couple who had two little girls, and they were looking for a maid or children's nanny, and they were very nice people. I said I would like to go there. By the time I left the convent, I was getting thirty bob, but this family were going to pay me three pounds week, give me my food and keep, and pay my insurance. There were two lovely little girls, one was two and the other was five, and I looked after the children, and did light housework. They had another woman who came and did the heavy work. They took me on holidays with them sometimes, and sometimes they let me take the children away on holidays, and I stayed there three years until I got married.

I met my husband through the Irish dances in St. Stephens Hall in Welling. He had come over from Kerry in 1936 and worked at the cable factory, Calenders. We married in 1950. An elderly couple had a big house next to the convent in Welling, and I was friendly with them, so they let us have two rooms there. We stayed with them for about fifteen months, and we bought a house of our own then in Plumstead. I have one married daughter and one beautiful grand-daughter, and they live in Somerset. My only regret is that they are so far away, but I visit them quite often. I sometimes wonder what life would have been like if I never left Ireland.

Pat Griffin (Julia's husband) and her daughter Margaret visiting Pat's family in Kerry

BRIDIE HARTIGAN

I am eighty five years of age, and I was born and bred in Newcastle West, County Limerick. My people had no farm, so I come from the poorest class in God's earthly world. I can't remember a lot about school, but I liked it alright, I was with the nuns.

When I was a girl, nearly as big as I am now, we all used to go to the bog in the morning, all of us singing our heads off. We would foot the turf, that is putting four sods of turf underneath, two on that and one on the top.

At Christmas the wren boys used to come round with the tamborines, the melodians and the flutes singing 'The wren, the wren, the King of all birds.' Then they would play for the dancing, and if you didn't dance, they would pull you out. That was St. Stephan's Day, the day after Christmas Day.

I used to go to house dances as a young girl. There was a farmer living in a thatched cottage, and we used to go back there to his place, and we had the music and the dances.

> At the crossroads we were dancing
> And the merry child was glancing
> To tell the fairy story
> Of Kerry long ago.

There was another verse to that song that I remember

We will say goodnight and kiss them
We go home and pray, God bless them
For the sweetness of our childhood days
In Kerry long ago.

Everyone who was there, they would get hold of you and pull you out.
We would dance the jig and the reel. You could have a laugh and a chat
and say what you liked.

When I was married I was nineteen years old, and I married a widower.
His people were from County Kerry, they were a very nice family. His
wife died and he had three children, but I never had anything to do with
them, they were always at their nanny's at the end of the street. I had
seven children, so there was a lot of work to be done. I used to do all the
washing, the shopping, the cleaning, I used to go picking up the sticks,
and then to the bog, and to the meadow, I used to go pulling the
potatoes. I used to do all kinds of work, you name it and I have done it.

We were living at Glin by then. I used to be called in to wash and lay out
the dead. Of course it was all different then, not like it is now. Then
there would be a wake, and people would come from all over the place
to the house, and the body would be laid out in the room. We would say
the rosary, and then they'd give out the snuff and the tobacco. We'd all
take a pinch of snuff, and the clay pipes would be filled and lit. I
remember the candlelight, and the praying. There would be tea and
sugar, and maybe porter or something stronger, whisky, for the men.
The next day I would wash the dead person ready for the funeral, they
would wear a brown habit just like the priest wears, you know. I used to
go to the funeral, and afterwards someone would say, 'here is your
wages'. And I might get five or six bob, or a gallon of milk, or a bottle of
whisky.

When I got married, I couldn't make the soda cake, I should have been
watching my mother making it, but I never did. So the girl next door
showed me how to do it, and I could then make a brown or white cake.
I'd get the flour, and a spoon or two of soda, a fist of bran made it very
nice, and the cream off the new milk used to be lovely at that time, or
the yoghurt, that's just as good. Then I'd make a hole in the middle and
mix the whole lot , then turn it out and flatten it. Then I'd make a cross
on the top, put it in the pan, and straight into the three legged oven. We
baked all sorts of things in those ovens. It all came out lovely.

During the war there was a scarcity of the tea and the sugar, you couldn't get a grain. So we'd brew the tea leaves again and again. You had to have a drop of tea. I used to do work for the neighbours, and they often paid me with the tea and the sugar, or a gallon of milk, and maybe a half a crown as well. As a general rule we ate potatoes but we had very little meat, except on a Sunday. If the local farmers had killed a pig they would give me my share of the puddings and rashers, they were very good like that.

Of course we had fun in those days, and when I had my own cottage, the neighbours would call round and we would have a house dance. I would give them tea and bread and butter, and maybe a cake I had made. We would have a great night, they would call to your house and you would call to their house. There's a crowd up the road from where I lived, the Mulligans, and I was there every night. They would say, 'Come on Bridie, give us a jig.' And I would be dancing and I would make all the lads dance, and they would be coaxing me, about four or five of them. They were great days. Sometimes Jim Callaghan would take Mary, my daughter and I to Puck Fair in County Kerry. We would go around and see all the things at the fair, and the Puck Goat of course, and have a fine time. Once I said to Mary, 'We will away here to this pub and have a drink.' Well we went in, and there was a huge crowd inside. Then some of the lads started pelting crubeens or pigs' feet at one another, oh it was wild, so we soon got out of there. There was always great music in the pubs and on the streets, so you could enjoy yourself and have a good day out.

My husband died when the children were very young, may the Lord have mercy on him. Life was very hard without him. Also I got no pension from the government, nobody did in those days. So I had to work even harder, the neighbours would call me to help them up on the meadow or on the bog. If I had the doctor in, and I did when my daughter had pneumonia, and then died, I had to pay for that. I paid in work elsewhere, although the doctor did not press me for the money. Clothes for all those children were a problem, but we managed. I'd go down to the drapers shop at Glin after I'd been paid and I'd take one of the children with me to be measured up for the trousers and all that. Sometimes the neighbours helped. Anyway when the child had something new, everyone would admire it. I remember one old farmer saying to my son Tom, 'My God Tom, haven't you got the great style, you have a new gansey on you.' If I'd bought them a blazer they would have said, 'Where in the name of God did you get that blazer?'

My son Tom was a devil when he was young, you know. He never wanted to go to school. I would leave him down at the crossroads and he would bolt. So I had to walk him to school every second day. The schoolmaster would come around on his bicycle and ask if Tom was at home, but he would be off away with his friend. One day Tom and his friend went to the school and put stones in the lock on the door, small stones, and the teacher could not open the door for school. Where he got the idea from, well I do not know. He is a man now and a great fellow altogether.

I have lived in this country this last fourteen years, all my children are living over here, but the step-children are in Ireland, one of them lives in my cottage. I have been back home, my son Sean took me for a holiday, and I didn't see a lot of changes. This country is made up of a lot of people I know, I still go out to the raffles and the bingo, and to the church, of course. The priests all know me, and sometimes at the church, one of them will come down in all his vestments and shake hands with me. There are a lot of Irish people over here, but I've found the English people are just as nice once they get used to you. I love Ireland, but while I stay here I have to like it here. My family are all here too. Like most Irish people, I'd like to be buried at home.

Bridie on holiday in Ireland

KATHLEEN HENRY

I come from Dublin. My parents both came from County Antrim, where my grandparents were small farmers with large families. My father worked in the Civil Service, and my mother worked in the G.P.O. as a telegraph operator, which was a skilled job. She had to leave that when she got married. I am one of five children. None of us are now in Ireland.

I had no idea what I wanted to do when I left school at eighteen. I was a very shy girl, very sheltered and shy. I did start work in an office, and then a couple of years later I was bored with that, so I came to England to do my nurse's training. A friend of mine was training in a hospital in Hastings, and that's where I went to do my genenal training. We were the only Irish girls there. That was in 1943.

My parents were very unhappy about letting me come over here. It was war-torn England, and they were afraid I'd be killed by bombs. To this day, I don't think I should have done it. My eldest brother had left home, but the others were there.

I was twenty-one when I came to England. Training was arranged by letter before I arrived. I must have written and told them what qualifications I had. They wanted a character reference, and a health reference. I think the schoolteacher did the character reference, and the doctor did the other. I had to go to the dentist for a certificate to say that my teeth were all right.

I was very happy most of the time in Hastings because I liked the work, I liked being active, I liked the patients and the other nurses, it was a bit

Kathleen (in the middle) aged five on a ladder against a peat stack in Carn Kern, County Antrim where her grandmother lived.

Kathleen's aunts and her brother and sister in Antrim with a pet lamb which is being fed from a kettle

like being at school. Most of the time I enjoyed it. We had bicycles and we used to go around the country. The trouble was, you often didn't get the same time off as your friend. There was one girl, her family were local people, and we used to go round and visit all her relations. They were very kind, they used to feed us. I'm amazed looking back, just how good they were.

It was a general training, so we did everything, not midwifery of course. I qualified in 1946 as a State Registered Nurse. Then I went to Liverpool and did my midwifery training. That was very interesting because you did six months on the district and you learned how people lived. There were a lot of Irish people in Liverpool, and it was great. The whole of Liverpool struck me as a very happy, generous place. The people would be living in those tiny little houses, and you would knock on the door, and they would say 'come in', and if they had anything to eat they would offer you some. They were fantastic people.

I finished my midwifery training just before the National Health Service came in. People had to pay a small amount and we had to collect it. The amount varied. The sister in charge would make an assessment and talk to the mother about it and say, 'Can you afford five shillings', or 'twenty-five shillings'. The district was organised from the Liverpool Maternity Hospital in the centre of Liverpool. Then there were six big old houses in different districts, and you were living in one of them and you worked from there. That way you were near the people you were visiting. We had an ante-natal clinic there, and the patients used to come in and the sister would discuss with them how much they should pay. A lot of mothers did not book, so you would be sent for when someone was in labour, and you'd never seen her before, so you were dependent on what preparations she had made.

As a pupil, you were attached to a midwife when you went around the district. She would go out with you to make an assessment and to see what was going on, and then depending on the circumstances, she might leave you and call back, if she had other people to see to. As you got more experienced you were probably left on your own. At night, we usually worked in twos, but not always.

Midwifery made me a bit nervous, knowing what things could go wrong, the responsibility of it. I knew that if I stayed on, I would really be on my own, and I didn't want that. So I worked in the hospital for a while as a hospital midwife, and then I went to Australia, to New South Wales, Tasmania. I worked in hospitals there. I just wanted to see the world a bit. We had an uncle who went to Australia, pioneers, and I had rather a romantic idea of what Australia was like.

I loved Australia, the country and the people, but I didn't like working there. In this country at that time, qualified nurses were given a lot of responsibility and they were really responsible people. It seemed to me that in Australia you were not treated like that. A doctor would come along and tell you when to take somebody's stitches out, and I felt that this was an insult. I stayed out there about three years, and then I came back. Oh it was easy to find work, too easy really. It was the early fifties when I arrived back in England, and there was plenty of work to be found.

I worked in the National Hospital in Queen Square. I was living in, which was one of the attractions of nursing to me. I was quite happy living in one room, and I went around with whoever I was friendly with at the time. We went to the theatre quite a bit, the Festival Hall, the Albert Hall, lots of places like that.

The work was very interesting. It was where they did the brain operations, but I found it depressing. You got all these people with brain tumors, little children. It was really intensive care nursing, but it wasn't called that at the time. It was really draining work.

After that I went and did my district nursing training, because it is a separate training after your general training. I went back to Liverpool to do that, and there again, you got into people's houses. You saw how they lived, even in the 1950s people would live a whole family in one room.

We used to go round on bicycles and we had a lot of visits to do. We couldn't spend much time with each patient. I remember an old man who had pneumonia and I was going to give him penicillin and all I could do was rush in, give him this penicillin and rush out again. I should have been able to give him a wash and make him comfortable, but I just hadn't time. His wife was there, but she was old and she couldn't do much. That was about the worst, most people were not as badly off as that.

Most of the children had a reasonable standard of health. However when I was health visiting, there would be families, even in the 1960s, where the children would have chronic chest diseases. Of course sometimes you would get a father who drank, and this was also when you got the children in a really bad state, because they just didn't have the money. I don't suppose they were properly fed. There was nothing anyone could do. I didn't like it because I felt so helpless.

I was working as a health visitor for some years, before I became superintendant of the nurses in the borough of Southwark, in the north of the borough for six years. In the 1970s I went back to health visiting and that is what I did until I retired in December 1980. I was living in a council flat in Peckham for ten years, and when I retired, I bought a flat in Belvedere where I live now.

I haven't been back to Ireland in a long while. My mother died in 1974. Until then I used to spend all my holidays there, because she was old, and I used to go to do whatever I could to help her. I have one brother, the others are all dead. It gets very difficult to go, the journey is difficult, and I'm not very well. I haven't been at all this year. The only family that I have left are in the north of Ireland, and I wouldn't go and live there. They are farmers in a very peaceful place, north of county Antrim. One of them lives near the Giants Causeway.

The bit of Dublin where I come from has not changed a great deal, but I found that Dublin itself had spread out a great deal. When we were young, we used to walk all over the Wicklow mountains, that was one of the things we did, and my father would come with us. We knew those mountains like the back of our hands. But now there are houses on them, people have built these beautiful houses on what was wild beauty. I suppose it's not ruined, but it doesn't look the same. I couldn't go up there anyway. I used to go on a bicycle or walking, but not now. When I go over, I have to stay in a hotel in Dublin. Well of course that's alright, you can find somewhere right in the centre, but unless you are feeling quite fit, it's very difficult staying in an hotel.

I joined the Irish in Britain Representation Group after reading about it in the Irish Post. That seemed to me to be the sort of thing that I would be interested in, and through that I joined the Irish Pensioners Group. I find with Irish people that you don't have to explain anything, they know, and you can just be yourself.

BRIGID KEENAN

I came from a family of twelve. I didn't live at my own house with my parents, I lived with cousins in the local village from the time I was nine. The mother had had a stroke and they wanted someone to be always there in case she needed anything. I would run errands for them and look after the shop when I came back from school. I went to the National school there, and got a very good education up to the age of fourteen.

They were business people and they ran an office of the Pearl Assurance. He used to pay out the health insurance cheques, and I used to help with that. It was also a land surveying firm. His daughter, my cousin, was a commercial teacher and she held classes in the school opposite where we lived. I looked after the shop while she was over there, and sometimes helped her bring the typewriters back in the evening.

My uncle was sacristan of the local church and so I used to help out a lot there. On Saturdays I did the flowers, and I'd lay up the altar. I used to admire the beautiful altar cloths. I taught myself how to crochet by looking at them. I used to ring the Angelus in the morning and sometimes in the evening. I loved helping out there. From the time I was nine to fourteen, my whole life was between the church and the school. I was in the choir. It was a way of life that I was happy with.

After I left school, I took a job as a cook general for a man and his daughter who ran a post office. It was a lovely job and they were very nice people. I had a boyfriend there and we had gone to a dance at the Palais and I had a date to meet him again, but he didn't turn up. I thought we were finished, and shortly after that I came to London. My sister took over my job in the post office.

I came over with a friend. We came for King George and Queen Elizabeth's coronation. It was on the spur of the moment, I think it was this girl's suggestion. She thought it would be better for us and probably we'd make a lot of money. This might have been right for her, as she was a little older than me, but really we were too young.

My family didn't know I was coming to stay. They didn't know until I was here and I wrote and told them. My mother was rather worried I think. My friend and I discussed it before we left. We would only accept indoor jobs, where we'd be secure. We agreed that when we got to London, we were going to look for hotel work. We'd made up our minds to do that from the very start. I don't think we had the money, anyway, to pay for lodgings.

When I went to my first interview at the Langham Hotel, the head house-keeper said to me, 'In this hotel, we are very particular about our girls.' We were the housemaids and we helped the chambermaids. We were training ourselves to become chambermaids because it was a high-class job in those days. She said, 'You dress like nurses.' I think she gave me the amount of money to buy the uniform. I had to go to Evans in Oxford Street to buy it. We wore a blue underdress with a white apron like a nurse's apron, with a white belt and a white cap.

'When you're in this hotel, you're a member of my own family', she said, 'I'll look after you.' And so she did. We were very very well looked after. There was another Irish girl there from Kerry, and shortly after another Irish girl arrived, Welsh girls and Scots. We had a lovely time, just like a family even to the chambermaids.

The chambermaids mothered us, because we were so young. I was nineteen. My chambermaid's name was Cissy. Cissy would be the one to pick up the tips, it wouldn't be me, unless some kind person handed me something, but they hardly ever did. You were more or less in the background. I had no direct dealings with the guests. But I did come face to face with some famous people. There was Rita Hayworth, she was on our floor for quite some time. She had a little Japanese maid. Cissy used to open the door and tried to go in, and she used to be sitting on the floor of the lounge of their suite, doing her hair up. I used to be fascinated. I wanted to see everything, I was very interested.

The chambermaids got ten shillings a week, and we got five shillings or 7/6d. They got tips as well. They tipped us. They gave us tips to share. We only had our specified time out. There was one very big night out at the Royal Albert Hall. It was a very special night and we all had to ask for special leave, late night passes. That allowed us to come home in the early hours of the morning if necessary. In all the hotels you've got the staff entrance, you never use the front door, where they have their special commissionaires. We arrived home by taxi from the Royal Albert Hall and the taxi man pulled up by the front entrance. Before we all got out, this commissionaire, in his white gloves and everything, came forward to open the taxi door. Of course when he saw us, he nearly dropped dead. Everybody being in a hilarious mood at that hour, we all rushed through the front door and up the stairs, and he reported us. We all had to appear before the head housekeeper the next morning, but she took it all in good part, and we didn't get any punishment for it. That would have been in 1937 sometime.

I was there for eight months. There was a very nice under-housekeeper there, and she went to the Ritz Hotel for an interview for a job herself. When she came back she said to me, 'The head housekeeper asked me if I knew anyone else, a nice girl that I could recommend to her for the 6th floor in the Ritz. Would you like to go there? But it's a strict secret, you mustn't tell anyone who told you.'

So I went for the interview. She was a Swiss Head housekeeper there then, and she took me on. I was in the Ritz for about eighteen months. It was very nice there too. I came into contact with King Boris of Bulgaria in the goods lift! We used the goods lift as it was more or less on our side, by the staff entrance. We had the builders in then and I thought he was one of the head men from the building firm. He had a black overcoat on, and an Anthony Eden bowler hat. When I got into the lift, he started talking to me and asked where was I off to now, and was I going to meet my boyfriend. I said, 'Yes, how did you figure that out?' 'Well', he said, 'a nice young girl dressed up like that could only be going to meet her boyfriend!' When he got out of the lift on the ground floor, the lift man shut the gate quick and he wouldn't let me out. So I said, 'What do you think you're doing? Let me out.' He took me down to the basement and on the way down he said, 'Do you know who you were talking to? That was King Boris of Bulgaria.' I said, 'Good luck to him then! Why was he on this lift. I'm the person supposed to be using this lift. Don't do that to me again!'

My sister forwarded me a letter from the young man I'd been seeing in Dublin. He told me the reason he had not turned up to see me that night was that he had broken his arm. Well, I started corresponding with him again, and he came over to London in 1937 and found himself a job as a waiter, and we were courting for a year.

In August 1938, I got fed up with London and went back to Dublin, working in a cafe there. I think the reason I missed Ireland at that point was that I felt lonely. I was going to daily work in the Regent's Palace Hotel and living out, so I only had a room to go home to. I think it got me down a bit and I felt it wasn't the life for me. When I was living in at the other hotels it had been like family life, the company was always there I began to feel a kind of pressure on me, a terrible loneliness.

My boyfriend followed me to Dublin and we were married there in St. Peter and St. Paul in October 1938. We were taken on as cook general and house parlourman at a very grand house in Dublin. They already had a chauffeur, a gardener, a needlewoman, a cleaner and a housekeeper. The housekeeper was young and very nice. She was very fond of me, and when I became pregnant, she pleaded with me to stay on and she would employ someone to look after the baby, but my husband refused point blank. He was keen to come back to London, so in 1939 we returned.

I never felt anything like the down-hearted feeling when I got back to London the second time. We had nowhere to live, and spent the night in a bug-ridden room in Camden, before we found one room in Charlotte Street for seventeen shillings a week. I had to find a place to have my baby, and the doctor said I'd left it very late to get myself a hospital bed. I ended up having my daughter in St. Pancras Hospital which was not what the doctor had wanted.

Shortly after she was born, war broke out, my husband joined up in the army, and I was evacuated with the baby to Bedford. My husband wanted me to be in Ireland when the bombing started in London, so he sent me and the baby to his mother in Dublin, where I spent two years from 1940. We moved back to England together in 1942 when he got a job in an aircraft factory in Bedford, but there was no fit accommodation for me. I was expecting my third baby and we were living in a little cottage with no facilities, so off I went again to Dublin, and my baby was born in the Rotunda Hospital in Dublin. We lived for one year in Cambridge in furnished rooms, and finally came back to London in 1944.

My husband found us a flat in Harrington Street. I came up in the November, 1944. We had all the upstairs of a big house in Harrington Street. It was a lovely flat, belonging to the London Midland Railway and it's a pity they were ever pulled down. In 1944, there were still flying bombs and rockets. I didnt realise this when I agreed to come back to London. By February 1945, I felt I couldn't take any more. I was taking the three children to Warren Street to sleep at night. I did that from November till January. Then one day, the ARP people came and said they had got tickets for me for the deep shelter at Camden Town. That was a hundred feet underground. So every evening, I took the three of them down to the deep shelter.

I had a terrible shock in Harrington Street one evening. I was getting them ready to take them to the shelter, it was about five o'clock. I gave two of them a cup of cocoa, and I was holding the baby on the settee, with a cup of tea near the gas stove, to drink before I went out. There was this dreadful bang. Both the children were blown accross the room. It was a rocket which burst in the air. If it had come down on us, we'd all have gone. Half of it fell next door. I saw it from the kitchen window, all the black smoke and everything in the air, with all the bits coming down. I watched the wall beside the window cracking. I got such a shock that afternoon that I don't think I got over it.

I've stayed in this area of London ever since. There were always a lot of Irish people around Camden Town. You'd be shopping in Camden, and they used to say, 'Oh there you are, they've lined up the Paddy Taxis for the night. Don't you know it's St. Patrick's Day today, and the Paddies will be all out around Camden Town tonight.' You'd hear people discussing it, and the'd give it out on the news the next day if a lot of arrests were made. But I have always found the English people very tolerant and placid about it. They'd say, 'Well you can't blame the poor fellows. After all they're living in rooms and they haven't got any family over here. And they only meet up in the pubs for their social life. You can't condemn them for it if they drink a bit too much.'

There's an Irish Centre in Camden now, which is very nice. You meet up with your own people and it brings you closer to Ireland. Some of us pensioners have signed up to have a lunch there every day. I spent an evening with all my family there when they had a county night, all the dancing and singing from a particular county.

When I went back to County Limerick, where I come from, after thirty

Oh, the shamrock,
The green immortal shamrock,
Chosen leaf
Of Bard and Chief
Old Erin's native
shamrock.

years, I had a terrible shock. One of my brothers died in 1981 and I went over for the funeral. I just couldn't believe the changes I saw. When I was there as a child, you'd see thatched white-washed houses, the doors open, the animals up to the old half front door, geese or ducks around the road and cattle grazing along the sides of the road, bare well-trimmed ditches, ponies and traps going along the roads, and people on bikes. The motor car has changed all that. I did notice that all the houses were beautifully done up, immaculately clean and flower boxes in the windows. They were solid little houses I suppose, and they've been extended and modernised, with bathrooms, running water, elecricity, carpeted floors, I was amazed.

An Irish identity is very important to me and to my children. They were very proud of it. And I am involved with a prayer group over here based at St. Aloysius which is a very Irish church near Euston. I go to Westminster Cathedral every Friday evening. Religion has always been very important to me. It has been my life and I don't know where I would have been without it. I always thank God for the faith my father and mother gave me. No matter what was going on in my life, I could flash back to my childhood. Day in and day out, my faith has never left me.

MOLLY KENNEDY

I was born in County Meath. It is known as the Royal County, because in Ancient Irish history the kings of Ireland would live on the Hill of Tara which is in County Meath and everyone is very proud of that. I was born in December 1917. I am the oldest of nine, six boys and three girls, and being the eldest I'd everything to do. I'd four brothers before I had a sister, so I had to look after the boys. I even had to polish the shoes, especially on a Saturday evening ready for church on a Sunday morning. I had to make sure there were laces and socks to go with the shoes. My mother used to go into town on a Saturday afternoon, to do the shopping and so on, and she'd expect all that to be done when she came home, not to mention scrubbing the table and chairs and the big dresser. It would all have to be spick and span when she came home.

We were right in the heart of the country. We were even three miles from the village. My father worked on a farm. We had a little bit of land, but you couldn't support nine children on it, so he worked on a farm and had a weekly wage from a farm, but had our own little bits and pieces. We always had milk, we had a couple of cows, a pig, plenty of eggs, and my father was always very good putting in the vegetables in the garden. We had the best of food, and where he worked he was allowed what we call 'tillage'. He'd be allowed so many drills of potatoes, so we were never hungry.

It was my father's own house. It was one of these old houses made of clay, but not thatched, it had slates. It was a beautiful little house. His father had built it. After years and years the council built a home for us on the same plot, but that was a lot later.

Mother was a very industrious woman and she reared chicken and turkey, all that sort of thing. She was very hard working, and used to stay up half the night sewing for us. At 1 o clock in the morning you'd hear the sewing machine going for us.

We had two bedrooms and a kitchen. Mum and Dad and all the little ones were in one bedroom, and as you got older you went into the other, boys or girls. If one of you got measles, you were all put into the same bed so you'd all have measles at the same time. The other girls were a lot younger than me, and compared to me they had a lady's life. I was the one who had to come in early and so on, but by the time they grew up and started going out, the parents were a bit more broad minded.

As I was off to school, 'When you get back in the evening, I want you to do the churning.' We went to a very good school that was three miles away, that's three Irish miles and they were very long Irish miles! We had to cross fields. The teachers were very good and the school was always in the limelight as regards school activities. It was run by the nuns and it was in the grounds of the convent. Our village school was run by lay people, two classes up and two down, girls upstairs and boys downstairs. I went there till I was about thirteen or fourteen, and then I was lucky enough to get a scholarship and that included board, so I went, and was in this convent for three years, in a local town.

We used to come home for the school holidays. I was treated just like the people who had paid the fees becuase I had earned mine. So that led up to when I was about seventeen, and then I went to do a bit of book-keeping for an aunt whose husband was ill. I had always had nursing in mind because my mother was in nursing and so were my sisters. I went into nursing in Dublin and I was there for a few years. I did enjoy it too.

I could have come over years before I did. When I decided to go to work in Dublin, I wanted to come over here to start my nursing, and a friend of mine even had an appointment for me at a hospital in Northampton, but my father wouldn't let me come. He said, 'If you go to that pagan country, you'll never darken my door again!' You did what you were told. But when I got married I was at an age when I made my own decisions. He was annoyed and disappointed, but that was it, it was my life then.

I got married in 1944, and came over to England soon after. I'd known my husband for years, as he was a friend of my brothers.

Molly with her brother

We came to London in the middle of rationing. I was home-sick but your pride wouldn't let you give in, you stuck it out. There were various reasons, first of all you were married, and then your pride made you keep the fair side out.

It was a terrible experience coming here as a young bride, because I didn't know a soul. I'd nobody in this country and my husband was at work all day. I'd go out and do a bit of shopping, plan and do the evening meal and washing and so on. This was in Lewisham. My husband was working in the building trade. The first job he had over here was erecting pre-fabs.

We came over with our broad Irish accents and everybody would look at you. When you went to the shops if you didn't see what you wanted on the counter or the shelf, you walked out. I was terribly self-conscious and could hardly ask for anything in the shops. Coming from the country, where we all had fireplaces, I never used gas in my life. There was so much to get used to.

I didn't feel I could carry on nursing over here because of the hours, so I was pleased to get a bit of clerical work. Then the babies came along, and I stayed home to look after them for a few years. Later, when the children were getting on a bit, I sat a Civil Service exam. and passed. I was in the Civil Service until I was sixty-five. It was really in the latter part of my life that I reaped the benefit of my early experience and education when I got into the Civil Service.

We went home every year, but then they started school and so on. It was always your mother you felt sorry for. My mother said, when I got married, 'I've lost her forever.' She missed me. I didn't know for a long time, but my brother told me she cried for a week. But she was so good, she was all the time waiting. Come St. Patrick's Day, there'd be the shamrock and the card.

It's nice to go home on holiday. We thought of going home, and there were one or two there who'd give us a little place, just a little bit of land where we could build a little house for ourselves. But, then, I couldn't pull myself away from the children. We'd a married son and daughter and five grandchildren. We thought well that's fine, we'd still be in the heart of the country. But my husband doesn't drive, so we'd have no transport. You wouldn't even be able to get to church from where we'd be living. The novelty would wear off and you'd be on your own. They all have their children and grandchildren around them, and we'd be on our own. We'd be back to where we started without a soul. Of people we know who have gone back, some have settled down and some haven't.

Even my daughter said 'You go mum, and we'd come and see you every year', and I said 'Yes, and how many times have you been to Ireland now? When your holidays come round now, you're off to Spain, Austria, Portugal, you've never been to Ireland since I took you there as a little girl, when we used to go back and forth in the school holidays. Dad and I would be left high and dry. We'd never see you or the children!'

It's because our families were so large and the farms and houses so small that we Irish are scattered all over the world. It's part of the Irish to travel. They couldn't all live in the nest, somebody had to get out. You just couldn't all live off those little farms. I know some people had big farms, but for most it just wasn't possible. We all left Ireland for the same reason.

Molly's brother scything

FRANK LENNON

Before I left Ireland, I was working on the farm. At twenty-two years of age, I could do all on the farm that had to be done, ploughing with the horses, raking with the horses, feeding the sheep and cattle. We had plenty of hard work. It was all hard work then, and I found a great change when I came to London. I'd been working out in the fields, and then I went straight over to London and started working inside.

The war had just finished and it was beautiful weather when I travelled over on the boat. I stood on the deck all the way over. My brother met me at Euston Station, and I couldn't get over what an immense place it was. I was going to work at the Cora Hotel in Southampton Row, where my brother worked. Coming straight from the open country in County Down, I was amazed at the height of the buildings in Southampton Row. I remember as we walked up the main staircase to the hotel manager's office, my feet were sinking into the carpet. I'd never walked on anything so soft before, indoors anyway.

I started as a house porter cleaning glass and washing down paint work. I'd never worked inside before, and I found it very hard in that heat. I lost a stone in weight. I never went above ten or eleven stone all the time I was there after that. It certainly kept you slim. And of course there was rationing, so you only got a small amount of food. Being in a hotel, I suppose we were not as badly off as some, and my brother was a waiter, so he could get us a bit extra. I remember there was a new thing called spam, beautiful stuff, which I'd never come across before.

I lived in at the hotel, and I gradually found my way round London. My brother worked evenings in the restaurant, so I was on my own. I went

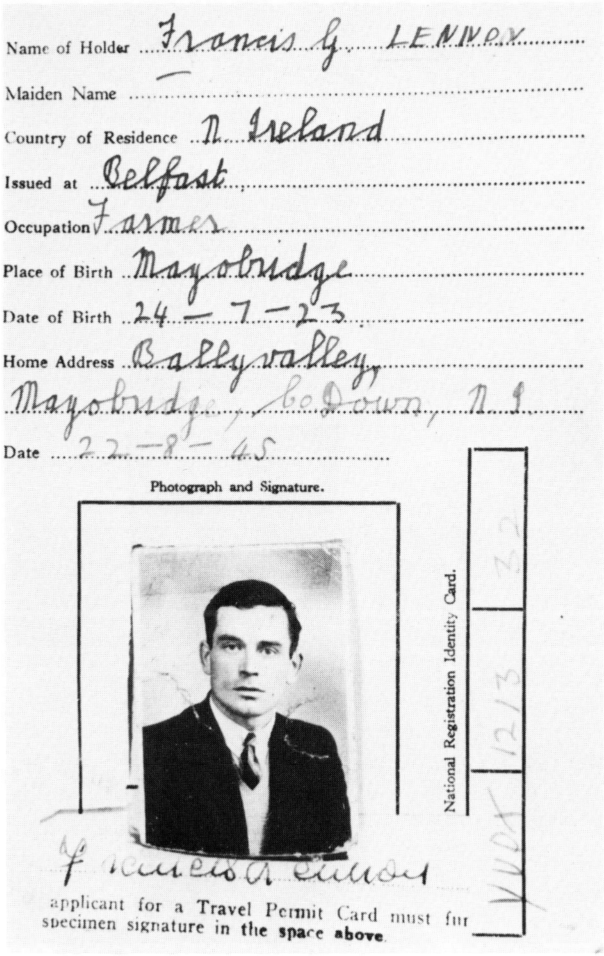

Name of Holder *Francis G. LENNOX*

Maiden Name

Country of Residence *N. Ireland*

Issued at *Belfast*,

Occupation *Farmer*

Place of Birth *Mayobridge*

Date of Birth *24 — 7 — 23*

Home Address *Ballyvalley,*
Mayobridge, Co. Down, N.I.

Date *22 — 8 — 45*

Photograph and Signature.

National Registration Identity Card.

applicant for a Travel Permit Card must fur
specimen signature in the space above.

Frank's entry visa

to the pictures a lot. They had news theatres where you could go in for a shilling and you had the news and cartoons for an hour or more. I walked all around the West End of London. Between Shaftesbury Avenue and Coventry Street, I got frightened by the ladies of the street when they approached me. I was afraid to talk to them and I was afraid to run away, so I walked rather fast. I didn't want to run in case people would think I'd done something and I would be apprehended. I didn't go through that way again.

After a couple of months, a friend of mine, Joey, arrived from Ireland, and then we started broadening our horizons. We found where the Irish dance halls were, and we used to go there in the evenings, a different dance hall every night. We'd travel all over to these dances, to Whitechapel and as far out as Surrey, and eventually there were about six or seven of us, Irish lads mostly working in the hotels, who used to go together as a crowd.

I had a brother in the Air Force and he was a prisoner of war with the Japanese in Java. When the war finished and the Japanese surrendered, my brother was expected to return home. But in September 1945, my parents got a telegram from the Red Cross telling them that my brother had died on a Japanese prison ship in September 1944. My parents were devastated with this news, and they sold up their bits and pieces and came over to England. My brother found them a flat in Somerstown near Euston, and I moved out of the hotel to live with them. I met my wife Kathleen in 1947. She came over with her sister and two friends to work as a chambermaid at the same hotel as me. When we were married in 1949, we moved into the top of the house where my parents were living. We remained in that house until 1966, by which time we had nine children.

I stayed in the hotel business quite a while. I moved up to become a waiter, and when the manager of my hotel moved on to a refurbished hotel in Upper Woburn Place, he took me with him and I stayed there for ten years until 1957, going from waiter to second head waiter and then head waiter. The work in the hotel was hard and you did a lot of hours. You had to be there at a quarter past seven in the morning, and you didn't finish till eleven o'clock at night. There'd be a break in the afternoon, so I'd go home and flop out. So that was a long day. It kept me slim. People kept saying to me, 'You're losing weight, but I knew I couldn't be losing weight all the time. I did look very thin and pasty, not having a lot of fresh air or sunshine.

By 1957, I felt I needed a complete change. I bought a kit of tools and went out as a carpenter. A fellow I knew said he was making good money at that and that I seemed reasonably handy, so I decided to try it. They were starting a new building in Euston and we were putting up shuttering for new columns. It was an absolute sun trap. It was beautiful weather in June, and I took my shirt off. I'd never worked with my shirt off before, and I got such a scorching with the sun that day, that I came home from work feeling terrible. I was suffering from sun stroke, and all the skin off my back peeled off. I was back at work the following day, but I didn't take my shirt off. That cured me of taking my shirt off!

Then I worked for years as a van driver, which was good money. I did quite well in that, but I developed back trouble. So I returned to waitering for another seven years. I did a good stint of clerical and supervisory work for a local council, before I retired at the age of sixty-five. Now I do three days a week in a hotel, working for the manager that I used to work for in the past. So you see I've turned full circle back into hotel work, after all the other bits and pieces in between.

Frank and Kathleen's wedding in 1949 with bridesmaid and Mark Fitzpatrick

I have been back home to Ireland, but not so very often because I was working hard and bringing up a family and I didn't have a lot of time. Now I find it's mostly funerals I go back for. Last year there were two. But all being well, next year we must go back for a good holiday. It's nice to go back and see everyone. I've a brother and sister there and my wife has family over there.

Some of our children have never been to Ireland. The older ones have been twice, and our oldest son went over this year for a week's holiday. But the younger ones haven't and we couldn't afford to take them there. They know nothing about Ireland or Irish culture. And when we go back, we find a lot has changed. There's much more money around than when we were young, and there are new people there who we know nothing about. But places don't change. The hills don't change, they're always the same. I still prefer going there to anywhere else. I love that adventure of setting off up the M1 and the M6 in the car, and getting the ferry from Stranraer to Larne and motoring then to Warrenpoint. It's really great, it's lovely, I really enjoy that.

Frank and Kathleen Lennon

JOSIE MACHIN

I was born in 1917, and I grew up in County Kildare, a place called Ferns Lock. My father was a station master and of course the rent wasn't very high because the house belonged to the railway. He used to get a bit of coal now and again for the fire, and then we had a lovely garden. My father was a good gardener. He'd started off as a gardener as a matter of fact out in Dalkey, working for some big Lord Somebody for two or three years from the time he was sixteen.

The garden we had it was down along this railway line and it was a hundred yards long or more, and we had everything in it. We'd the most beautiful kind of a hilly place there and it was all full of roses and lillies and all sorts of sweet pea and every kind of beautiful flowers you could mention. And then we had lovely strawberries, we had raspberries, we had blackcurrants,we had gooseberries and then we had the vegetables. We'd have well, everything you could think of in the line of vegetables: carrots, celery, parsnips, cabbage, peas and beans, everything you could think of in the line of vegetables. And then at the very end of the garden we had the potatoes, rows and rows of potatoes. We were never short of food, so we only had to buy meat and bread and butter. We had a cow down there as well.

We went to school in a little town nearby called Kilcock. We were allowed to be late because the train came about quarter to ten at our station and it wouldn't arrive at the next station where we went to school till about ten o'clock and then we had a half a mile up the road to go down from the station to the school, so it was always nearly half ten anyway before we got into school. And we had to stop by in the evening then for half an hour, when we used to do our catechism and our bible.

The school was run by the nuns and they were very strict. My God I got plenty of walloping there. Walloped with those pointers for not knowing your catechism or not knowing your sums or not being able to spell or something like that, silly things, they wouldn't do it now.

Some of the lessons we learned through Irish. But not everything, only one or two classes of Irish we'd have you know. I could read and write it all right, and I could spell, and I could write a composition in Irish, but I was never too keen on it really.

My mother was nearly forty when I was born and she had far more education than I ever had, even though I don't suppose she went to school half as long as I did. She was able to read and spell and sew and knit and do sums and me father was too. My father was a gorgeous writer. Looking back now, I think the nuns weren't all that keen on teaching us, they were a bit stuck up in a way, because they only went for the people who had the money.

If you had a big farm, or your father was a major or a doctor or something, a big noise, the nuns'd be around them. But the poor unfortunate ones, they never got a look in hardly. That kind of thing went on and that's why me mother never liked it, she hated it in Kilcock.

You see the nuns wanted to be in with all the snobs. You see there were hoity toity folk there, some of them had race horses and big farms and they'd be bringing in the nuns bags of this and boxes of that and loads of oranges, apples and a few sweets and fruits and this type of thing, they went for them.

Some of the kids wouldn't come to school every day and they were a bit behind. You had to do a bit of an exam to pass from one class to another, no matter what your age was. So you might have children from eight to twelve years in the same class depending on their brains.

I remember my first communion. At that time you had to fast from twelve o'clock the night before, there was no such thing as having your breakfast and going to communion like you have now. You had to get up and go to the 8 o'clock mass and I had to walk three miles before I got there, so I'd fast from twelve, we'd be up at about six and that nearly killed me. There was an old chap up the road who had a pony and trap and he said if we wanted to go to early mass he'd bring us in the trap. He had an old housekeeper, so myself and my sister Nan, we'd go up in the trap with them. At our first communion we were taken into the convent and we got a big breakfast there, bacon and eggs and sausages and fried up food, nice breakfast. We had to walk home then after that, the three miles.

If they saw you dressed up as a young communicant they'd give you a couple of bob in your purse or whatever you had, a little bag with a string on it and they'd come over and say, 'There's a shilling', or two shillings or if you were lucky you'd get a half a crown. Very few people would give you a pound. If they saw you and they knew you they'd give you a couple of bob and you might have two or three pound at the end of the day and you thought you were a rich woman. I'd give it to me mother and say, 'Buy me a new pair of shoes or something.' I gave it to my mother to keep it for herself as well if she wanted it. At that time kids weren't so fond of money, they liked to share it out.

I made me confirmation in Kilcock. A one street town, the convent was very nice, but the nuns were damned strict you know. They were really old fashioned at that time. The Bishop would only come down once every three or four years for confirmation and I was kind of young to be confirmed. Everyone was in white frocks and veils, and one trying to outdo the other, you know.

I had a nice long white frock, patent shoes and white socks. I can see the frock, with three or four flounces on it, and a veil with flowers going around the crown of it, and my sister was dressed the same. She was confirmed at the same time. The two frocks we had were the very same make and all that. My mother was a very good sewer and she had a machine. She made the dresses.

Everyone was shivering in our shirts in the cold weather, I mean you were used to wearing a coat and a cardigan and of course we were so fanciful we didn't want to wear a cardigan, we wanted everyone to see us in the white frocks.

We were so full of giggles, and we were in the chapel and I'd be looking round at her and I'd make faces or something and the two of us, we were shaking with the laughing, you know that kind of thing when you get into a fit of laughter and you can't stop. We had the whole place laughing. We were there ages and ages, and the bishop gave a sermon and we got all this oil on our heads for the confirmation.

We were examined by the bishop. He'd just say, 'You boy, what is the meaning of the redemption?' or 'What is the meaning of exorcism?' or

'When did our Lord rise from the dead?' (some question like that you know). I was shaking when he started asking the questions. I was in such a fit of giggles I don't know whether I said the right thing or not. He pointed out who he wanted. You wouldn't know who was going to be asked the questions. Some of them was never asked at all. I was asked, I forget what it was, some silly thing I suppose. I think I knew it anyway.

We had a confirmation party: sandwiches out in the country, nicely made sandwiches, whereas if we were in our own home we'd just get two bits of bread and put a bit of meat in and go off and eat it. But sitting down at a nice posh table, cups all along the table, and all sorts of fruit and jelly and custard and all kinds of sweet cakes. A lot of parents of the kids brought sweet cakes and made fancy stuff for the party.

There was ten of us in the family, although five of them were working during the time I was growing up. There were three girls and two boys during my time, so it wasn't very easy to keep going with five kids, with only father's wages.

Oh Christmas was marvellous. My older brothers and sisters were away working. I had a brother Tom on the railway, the best brother that was in the family. Tom used to come home every Christmas and that's where all our presents used to come from. You see me mother and me father would hang our stockings up and we'd get plenty of sweets and oranges and apples and things in them, but me brother always used to bring us something lovely.

Tom would come off the train and there'd be drinks and lemonade for us and Guinness for the adults, and they'd be sitting down having a chat and we'd have a big meal when he came home. My older sister Kitty used to take the cases and put them down in the bedroom so that no one would be at them, but my brother Peter, he's two or three years younger than me, he was a little devil, and he'd always know that when Tom was coming home there'd be something good in the cases you see. Everytime that Tom came for Christmas, Peter went down and he opened the cases and rooted every bloody thing out and he'd know what was in them before anyone, and then one night my sister Kitty went down and she caught him at it and he got a damn good trouncing.

Tom used to bring beautiful dolls for my sister Nan and me. One year he bought Nan and me a little shop with the little jars, and we put them on a table and pretended we were doing business. For the boys Tom would bring fishing rods or bats and balls. He'd have two cases packed and

Josie with her mother, sister Mary and brother Peter on Ferns Lock Station platform

113

then he'd have something for me mother and father. He'd bring paper hats and chocolates and things that we wouldn't normally get around our house. We had all good grub and everything, so we were always looking out for Tom.

At Christmas we'd have a kind of a concert at school. We used to be singing in the concerts, songs like the Three Old Maids from Lee, I can't remember the words of it now, but there were three of us in it and we had big bonnets and long frocks. We were three young maids first and we'd stand on the stage and we'd sing the three young maids from Lee and then we'd sing another verse where we were getting older and then we'd have to turn round our backs and we had the old faces behind us on the bonnets, so it was then the Three Old Maids from Lee, you see, and we'd sing that as well.

We always had plenty to eat and drink for the Christmas because we were in Ferns Lock, Kildare, which was three or four yards along the road from County Meath, where there was colonels and majors and all big shots living that was in the 1st World War, Major Winters and Colonel Purdon and Mr Love, he was a doctor, big people and then Colonel Bumfort was another old fella, had a big castle nearly as big as Buckingham Palace and they were all wealthy people who had race horses and lots of land and cattle.

Josie on violin, Nan on the melodeon and sister Agnes holding the hat

Where we were, there was a crossing gate, and from the signal cabin my father used to open the gate by turning a wheel, and we children used to do it as well. If there was a train coming, and they couldn't cross over the gate, they'd have to wait till the train went by, so every year they used to come along and they'd bring us in a side of beef, another one one or two turkeys another one a couple of legs of lamb and you'd always get something from someone, maybe a bag of potatoes although we had our own, they were always very decent, very good neighbours to us just because we used to open the gates for them, kind of a thanksgiving thing.

In Ferns Lock there were about five houses around and they were mostly herdsmen and farming people and one or two railway people, a railway cottage that a signalman was in, and the grand canal ran behind our house and a lock keeper there on the other side of the road, but the lock keeper was an old man, Jim. His wife Mary Ann used to be out shouting and bawling along the canal banks at the cows and at the turkeys. We used to pester the life out of this old couple.

We used to have turkeys. We had a couple of hen turkeys but no cock turkey. Me and my sister Kitty, we brought our turkeys over to Mary Anne's house one Sunday morning when she and Jim had gone to mass. We went into the kitchen and we thought that Mary Ann's cock turkey would tread our hens and we'd be all right, we'd have young turkeys. Sure the bloody old cock turkey she started to fly around the bloody house and knocked everything over. Old Mary Anne's turkey flapped its wings and knocked over all the Delft and all the bloody stuff that was on the shelves, so of course we nearly died. We had to clear up and come out, bringing our turkeys with us. Then when she came home from mass then she comes over to our house and she says, 'My God I don't know who was over in my place, the whole place is upset. I don't know whether the turkey must have flown up on the shelf or something.' And we were busting laughing.

My brothers were football mad and of course you know what Gaelic football is in Ireland, well this family up the road there were three girls and three brothers, three fellas would come out, my two brothers they'd be kicking football, of course the girls used to go with them as well. I'd be put in the goal sometimes, and I remember one day the ball hit me it came with such force that I nearly rolled into the river. But then we had camogie, like hurley only the girls play it. We used to have a little bit of a team of our own.

My brother Peter and I used to go fishing in the river and we'd catch all these little pinkies and widgets, get a pin and twist it like a hook, put a bit of thread on it, or a bit of fine twine and an old stick you'd pull out of the hedge and we used to sit on the banks of the river and we'd pull in all the little pinkies, put them in a jar, bring them home, and give them to the cat.

In the evenings, especially in the winter my mother would be sitting at the side of the fire knitting and sewing and that. Kitty would be the other side, me father would be reading the paper and talking politics and this and that. Then my sister Kitty she was going with a fella by the name of Joe Flannagan, he's still alive, and he used to come out from Kilcock on the bicycle every night and come over to our place and he'd sit round the fire with us and they'd be talking all sort of politics.

Sometimes there'd be card games, whist, beggar my neighbour, snap and that kind of thing. Then there'd be a big table in the middle of the kitchen with a big lamp or two on it and Kitty and I we'd be writing our letters and drawing our pictures and painting our bits and pieces. We'd always be in bed about 9 o'clock of the night though. Father wouldn't let us stay up, sometimes we'd say the rosaries during Lent and the month of May. We'd kneel down and say our rosary every night before we went to bed as a family.

When I was about ten, my father was transferred down to Maam Cross in County Galway. It was completely different. We all loved Galway. We met all our new neighbours and they were so nice. Well I mean Kildare is one of the richest counties in Ireland you might say, very well tilled and plenty of fat cattle and good land, big houses and castles and wealthy people which were more or less English that came over there in troubled times and stayed there. I was glad to get away from Kilcock, I didn't really like it at all, none of us liked it. The only one that liked it was Kitty beause she had a boyfriend there you see.

At Maam Cross the school and the church was all one. I went to school there for a year or two. There was only the one teacher, Mrs. Ridge, and she was a very good teacher. There was about ten or a dozen pupils. There was a crowd that used to come from across the mountains, the Barratts, mostly fellas, one girl and three boys and then there was the O'Briens, they used to come down from another mountain and they came down on donkeys. At lunch time we used to be out riding on the donkeys. They used to tie them at the back of the school and we'd be having a ride up and down the road with the donkeys. It was great.

Last train leaving Maam Cross Station April 29th 1935

I was in Dublin during the war. When I left school I went to the technical school in Dublin and I left there round about seventeen, and I got on the railway as an apprentice to the telegraph. All I was earning was ten shillings a week for two years before I got promotion. None of the old ones at that time used to get pensioned out, you didn't get pensioned out till you died. They left them all on the railway until they died, except if you got married you had to leave, but all the old ones that was on it they never got married, there must have been about 20 old ones. There were three sisters in Mullingar and there was two or three lassies at Athlone that never got married so they held the jobs from the time they were born nearly.

When I started working, I was doing the telegraph, morse code, on the railway. My friend Rita Quinn was a telegraphist at another station down the line, and we used to send messages to one another on the dots and dashes. Our real work was to wire all the cattle specials and sheep specials, and if there was a parcel sent or a bundle of papers there'd be a message about that, you know.

Well Rita was dance mad, and from the time she was thirteeen or fourteen she was going to all the dances she could get her leg at, but I never bothered me head. I never wanted to go dancing funnily enough. I'd dance at home, doing jigs and reels, putting the gramophone on and I'd plenty of records. But the first dance I went to was in Dublin. My sister Nan was in Dublin working in a drapery shop, making all the kids' clothes for a Mrs. Ryan that owned the shop, and I was staying with her. Nan was fairly on with the dancing, she liked it. Every Tuesday night they'd go to the Bamba and then Friday or Saturday night, they'd go to Barrys and then some place else Sunday night.

Rita was coming up to do relief work in Dublin and I met her at the station. She was asking me all the questions about the dances, and would I go to a dance with her. I said, 'No, but I'll bring you down to a dance and put you in the hall, and I'll go home then.' Anyway, I met her in the station, got her digs in the same street where I was, and she says, 'You must come to the dance.' I said, 'All right. I'll bring you down to the hall. My sister is down there still, and all the ones she goes dancing with. I'm not going to the dance Rita, but I'll leave you down there, introduce you to me sister and she'll look after you.' So that's what I done.

But when I went down to the dance, even though I didn't put any frock or nothing on me, just went down in me old clothes, they persuaded me. I went to the fellas on the door and I said, 'There's a sister of mine in there, and this girl wants to go dancing, but I'm not going dancing.' 'Why wouldn't you?' says the man on the door. 'Of course you're coming dancing.' So he let us in for nothing. So I saw me sister out on the floor dancing and I beckoned to her. I said, 'This is a friend of mine from Athlone, a telegraph clerk and you're to look after her and put her on the bus or the tram to come home.' So Nan says okay, so I was walking out and she says, 'Well, you're in now and you might as well stay in.'

The fellas were all standing at the end of the hall, and the girls sat down around the sides of the hall and then the fellas would go over and say, 'Would you like this dance miss?' If you went to the dance regular you'd get to know the whole lot of them and you'd never be short of dances and you wouldn't be left standing like a fool. Well, this fella comes over to me and takes me out to dance. I said 'I'm sorry I can't dance, I was never at a dance in me life before, I can't dance.' He said, 'You'll never learn if you don't try.' So we got around the floor anyway and he came over every bloody dance nearly and he had a pal with him, the two of them danced us all night. I went with him for eight years after, but I didn't marry him. When I got the hang of the dancing I couldn't stay at home. He said I danced his legs off for ever after!

I was in Dublin when the bombs went off yeah. We used to hear the German planes going across the country every night going on to Belfast, because Belfast was fairly badly bombed. One night in particular I was in bed and I think it was a Friday or Saturday night, and we heard these things buzzing, going across and we used to say then, 'Well that's the planes going on to to Belfast now. I wonder when they will be coming back.' They'd be up there about two or three hours and then you'd hear them coming back again.

One particular night there was this buzz over the whole city you might say and it seemed to be in the one spot all the time and the next thing was this blinking bang, the whole city was struck, so of course we all were shivering in our shoes, we thought we were finished. The old house I was staying in, well even if heavy lorries passed it used to shake, so you can imagine, I thought the whole thing was coming down on top of me. I was in bed on me own and in the flat on me own. There was people living upstairs in flats as well, and of course they all ran for the streets in their nightshirts and raced out to the Dominican church across the street and all the people round the whole area ran to the priest and the church and they all went in there and started praying. I stayed in me flat. I took me beads out alright, I've never prayed as hard as I did then. I was eating me rosary nearly.

I was promoted then and made clerk in charge in Mullingar. I was in charge of five, six girls and I was there for fourteen years. I was the belle of the ball down there you might say, I was here there and everywhere. But Mullingar is a very flat town, the people are very flat. In any part of the middle of Ireland the people are flat! They haven't got the same enthusiasm or the niceness about them as round the coast of Ireland where you've got the hills and the fields and the mountains and the sea. Near the sea the people are quite different I think.

Then I got fed up and I left. All my friends I used to dance with were married over here, and I had no one more or less. So I said, 'Ah to hell with this! I'll pack me bag and go.' They were asking me to come over here, five or six of my friends that I used to pal around with down there, they were all gone, so I said, 'To heck with it, I think I'll make a move. I had a good job and all and I packed it all up and came over here.

They were down in Bexhill, these girls they had a house in Bexhill there was about five of them in it and they were working in the hotels down there. They were well off and they were getting on well. So I went straight to them to Bexhill first and I stayed there for six months but I couldn't get a clerical job of any sort. That was 1960. Not the type of job I wanted. I could have gone into the hotels and done waitressing and washing. I done that for about three or four months and came to London. I went down to Kings Cross, and I was recruited onto the railway there and went in there and was doing my old job, teleprinting. I was taken on straight away. Oh I had a great job, I got promoted, I was only six months in Kings Cross when I was promoted. I started off from scratch getting eight or nine pound a week which was good money that time, then I was getting thirteen or fourteen pound you know and it was going up and up all the time.

I got this little room, a bedsitter in Tufnell Park, two pound ten a week it was only. I had my own cooking things and everything in it and could bring my friends in and have a drink and go out and have a drink if I wanted so I was quite happy there. Then I met my husband. He was an Englishman and a foreman on the railway there then. We got married in 1969, and soon after that we got a council flat in Camden, and I've been here ever since.

I think no matter how long you're in England you never have the same atmosphere at all as there is in Ireland. I mean you've got the friends there, the jokes you make in Ireland everyone understands them. You make jokes over here, and they don't seem to know what you're talking about, and of course they make jokes I don't understand either. I wouldn't laugh at some of their jokes at all. And then if you go to Ireland and you go into a pub or even a bus or railway carriage, everyone seems to say, 'Hello, how are you?' Whereas you can be two hundred years in England, if you're in a train they wouldn't even look at you.

MARY MASON

I come from the South, County Kerry. I came over here very young when I was eighteen, and I've been here about fifty years now. I came from the country and when I was a kid, there were long summer days and we used to play in the hay. We had a little farm and we'd gather the hay for my father. That is Ireland for me, that is what I remember of Ireland.

We had to learn Irish at school, but our teacher was not much good at teaching it because he barely spoke it himself. When we spoke to my grandfather and grandmother and we'd say 'a fine day' in Irish, they didn't know what we were talking about, because it was so different. My parents could speak Irish but they never spoke to us in it. They only spoke Irish with the old people that came in.

I'd left school at fifteen and I worked for a family in Cahersiveen before I came here. It was very hard work because it was a very busy place. I looked after the children. The family had a shop, a bakery, and they used to do teas, upstairs and downstairs. On market days it was very busy, because there was a lot of people coming in for teas and lunch. On fair days the boss looked after the four children upstairs while I waited on table, made the teas, brought in the bread from the bakery, ran backwards and forwards. I used to be really tired. There was another girl who helped there, but she left, so I took over her job, and they got another girl to look after the children. But the new girl hadn't much idea and the children knew me so well, so I still had to do things for them. I used to be run off my feet.

I started about eight in the morning. There was no day off. I was paid £1 a month. The boss kept telling me that was good pay, the best pay in the town. I was free to go out after eight or nine o'clock in the evening, but I was too tired. I might have a stroll up the town for an hour.

After I'd been there for three years, my cousin came from America and was then going to come on over here to England. She came into town one day and said would I like to go to London, and I said yes. I didn't see her for a while, and I thought, oh well, she's probably forgotten about it. I had a new boyfriend anyway, who I liked very much, and he was very nice to me so I thought I couldn't leave!

Then my brother came into the town and said that my cousin was going to England at the weekend, and that if I wanted to go I should come home. He didn't want me to leave home, but I thought, 'Now's my chance. If I don't do it now I never will.' So he said, 'Are you going?' and I said 'Yes.' 'Then you'd better go home tonight and have a few days off.' 'I can't,' I said, 'I can't, I haven't told the lady yet.' When I told the boss I was leaving, she was very cross with me and I came home the next day. I was the first one to come and I thought it would be lovely here.

The very first job I had over here was in a guest house in St. John's Wood and we were waiting at table. I had my sister out from Ireland then, and we were doing the housework. The husband and wife were very nice. She even wrote to my mother and told her how happy we were, and how pleased she was with us and so on. They did have little funny ways. Those guests that paid the most money got the best dinner and got served first, and it was most awkward because everyone else would be wondering what we were doing. Often we were so embarrassed we didn't bother, and just went along the tables putting the dinners down, so sometimes those who were paying more wouldn't get the best dinners.

I was there for about a year. Then my friend Nora got a job with a Russian Countess in St. John's Wood in London, so I went there too. The Countess was alright but she was rather mean. I think we got a pound a week. She said she had to be mean because she'd lost all her money in the Russian War. Her husband was much older than her and he could not work in this country because he was too old. She had two children, but they were away at boarding school. They never came to the London house, they went to their home in Suffolk. She used to go away a lot, because she had this house in the country.

Countess Benckendorf was a harpist, and she played under the name Maria Korshinska. I used to keep a check on her harp to see how many strings were missing. She said I was an expert at that, she was nice to me really. I used to go to Elstree with her. She didn't have anyone to take the harp, it would cost too much money, so she had her own car, and she used to make me sit in the boot and hold the harp up! Of course it was very uncomfortable, but I was young and I suppose I didn't feel it. I had to hold the harp a certain way, otherwise it would be banging, so the harp used to get there in one piece.

I went with her another time to Folkestone. She was playing in a Promenade Concert. It was my first day at the seaside, I was all on my own as I couldn't stay up in the concert listening to her, so I went down to the seaside. It reminded me so much of home. There were winding stairs going into Folkestone sea, and where I came from was very near the sea, but very hard to get down to it, because there's no road and it's all briars. It was a nice day, but I was really tired. I don't think she took the harp that day, I think there was one there already. I think she took me for company. I was her companion at times. She'd often ask if we were on the right road, and I'd say yes, even though I couldn't see in the dark as she was driving too fast!

The Countess was very neat and she always wore black. She said she hadn't much money, so she kept to black. She used to wear a black skirt and a black jumper. When she had to go out for something big, she wore a black frock. She used to have her hair parted in the front, combed down and back, and no mattter how often she went to the hairdressers, it didn't make any good impression on it, because her hair never took any sets. It stayed the same. She was rather attractive.

She used to go to the country every weekend she was free, because she had a house in Suffolk and would go there to her husband. She didn't like us to go out. She wanted us to be in to take any phone calls about engagements that came in while she was at the B.B.C., because that was her living. Sometimes she'd be away for hours, and I couldn't bear to be inside when I thought of the dances, so I used to go out. One evening, I sneaked out to go to a dance. I was so carried away that I forgot about the Countess. And then my heart was up to my mouth. Would she be inside before me?

We used to go to a lot of Irish dances, and meet a lot of Irish people in the dance halls. There would be a few accordian players, and we would have the Irish sets and the Irish reels, barn dances and waltzes, things

Mary Mason (right) with her friend Nora who also worked for the Countess

like that. There was one other girl working there, and when the girl left, she didn't replace her because she said she couldn't afford it. When the other girl left, the Countess didn't want me to be on my own and she asked my sister to sleep in.

My sister had her own job, she worked in a factory. One night, my sister was out with her boyfriend and I was out with some boy. We used to leave the back door open, because if the Countess was in she'd lock the door and chain it. There was a curtain in front of the back door so you'd never know it was open. We'd come in the back door and steal upstairs. My sister was stealing up before me. She suggested that I take off all my clothes so then if the Countess found me going upstairs, I could say I was up for a glass of water.

We all slept on the same landing and there was a loose board. So we got to the landing, and the board creaked. There was this shriek, 'Who is it? Who is it?' and nobody answered. I jumped into bed. At that time we used to wear hats, and I whipped off my hat and put it under the bed. My sister was sitting in a chair downstairs when she went down. 'What's this?' she said, 'What's going on? Did I hear you coming in?' So my sister said, 'Tonight is dog racing at White City and I couldn't get a bus home.' So the Countess said, 'Well, it's not fair on your sister, she has to be up in the morning and you're keeping her awake at night.' I waited till she'd gone and then got out of bed to undress and get into bed properly. In the morning she said to me, 'I don't think it's fair on you, your sister coming in so late.'

I was there till I got married. I must have been there about four years I suppose. I used to go back to Ireland every year and I used to stay a whole month, with the children. Once my mother died, I didn't go so often. My home isn't there now, and my sister is married and in a different part.

GERRY McTAGUE

I come from a little town called Ballinamore, in County Leitrim, near the border. My father worked in the local railway works. He was a fitter, a turner, and that was the only works within a fifty mile radius. It was a poverty-stricken area, mainly small farms. Most of the chaps I went to school with, they brought a couple of slices of home-made cake with them for their lunch and they were very poorly clad. Always clean, spotlessly clean, and they often walked five or six miles to school.

I hated school. We had a teacher there and he was beastly to us. I learned afterwards that he had a drink problem, but we didn't realise this at the time. We couldn't learn from him because we were too scared. We were scared stiff going to school every morning.

He'd hit you for little things that got on his nerves, like if you couldn't do the sum that he'd asked you to on the blackboard. If you hesitated, he didn't say anything, he just punched you on the back of the head and he seemed to take a delight in beating you, you know. He was aggressive, he used to grind his teeth and squeeze his fists together in temper.

He was the beginning and end of everything that happened in that school and our parents looked up to him because he was very Irish in his thinking and his approach to everything. He tried to beat the Irish language into you with his fists and he had no patience with you if you were slow to learn.

A lot of what he was trying to get over to you was above your head, and the result for me was that I never got to grips with maths. I could never

ever grasp it because I missed the first basics, and I could never catch up on it again. The fear that he held over me prevented me. He'd only to look at me and I'd shiver in case he'd come and stand behind me and start belting the back of my head which he did regularly. He had a habit of getting his knuckles into your ears and lifting you up by your ears and when I look back on it he was a beast really. But today they have a park named after him and think he was a marvellous man, but they don't know what it was like to be his pupil.

I'll give you an instance. One day I had to visit the loo, and I was cutting my name in the door with a pen-knife, my initials you know. There were hundreds. Everyone's name was out on that door. But suddenly I got a punch on the back of my head. He said, 'Get up, get up, get up to school.' When I got there, he put me up on top of the desk on a level with him, and he just sent me flying from that desk. I fell on the floor and hit my head against the wall, and I was lying there senseless for five minutes. He beat me again when I came round. He used to just go into a frenzy, lose all control. I was afraid to tell my parents because they wouldn't believe me. They'd say, 'If you didn't deserve it you wouldn't get it.' That was the parents' attitude then.

I have to wear glasses now since then. The doctor in the eye and ear hospital in Dublin told my mum that it was because of blows to the head that my eyesight was badly affected. I had to have an operation over my right eye from an optic nerve being displaced and the doctor said that was probably caused by a violent punch to the head. Well the only one who ever punched me on the head was this master.

There was a small element in the class who he never touched at all, who he was very nice to, and they were the people from the right side of the track sort of thing, the shop keepers' sons and doctors' sons and rich people's sons, they were never touched. They were all in the back seats in the classroom and they were never touched. But we were beaten and punched and kicked by that teacher. I don't want to exaggerate, but it stays with you for the rest of your life. And it hinders you from learning. I just wanted to get away from school. The quicker you got away, the better. Through him I took a terrific dislike to school, I hated the thought of going to school.

Years later I met another of his ex-pupils. He'd served with the 8th Army during the war and after the war he got in touch with me here in London, we were having a drink one night and he said to me, 'Gerry there's something I'd like to do,' he said 'I'd like to go back and find that old teacher and just give him a taste of what he gave us, just let him see what it felt like to be the wrong end of a very heavy punch.' He told me that when he was abroad with the 8th Army he used to lie awake in the desert at night and think of what that master did to him you know. I said, 'Don't be ridiculous.' But eventually we went back there, and this chap picked an argument with him deliberately, told him then who he was and what he was doing there. He said, 'And now you're going to find out what I felt like when I was at the end of your brutal punches when we were kids and couldn't defend ourselves.' So he struck him there and then and sent him flying, because of course the teacher was rather old then you know. That soldier chap died soon afterwards but he was very happy that he was able to do that. Today the way they speak about that master you'd think that he was a local saint or something.

I left home when I was thirteen because of an incident that happened in the local church. I was in the Catholic Boy Scouts and we were supposed to be an example to the local youth when we went to mass. Another chap and myself were whispering together about where we were going that afternoon and the priest happened to see us. He was preaching at the altar and he left the altar and walked down through the church, came up in the gallery, stood over the two of us. He told us both to stand up, and shouted at us then from the top of his voice. 'If you're the kind of Catholic boy scouts we're breeding in Ireland, then may God save Ireland. Now leave the church.' So we had to walk out of that church, like being drummed out.

When we got back to the local hall where the scouts were based, they told us that they'd had a quick meeting, and had decided that we had to apologise to the priest for our despicable conduct. Well my friend had to apologise because his parents were politicians, and the father was very concerned about holding on to the local vote. Well, if you fall out with the local priest in a small Irish country town, you lose a lot of the local voters as well, so he had to apologise. His parents later told me that if it hadn't been for this, their son would not have made an apology. But my father wouldn't allow me to. He said, 'No, you didn't do anything that Christ wouldn't like if he was on the altar. If Christ had been on the altar that day, he wouldn't have come down and told you off.' I was court-marshalled by the local scouts commissioner and dismissed with ignominy.

Well after that I was being ostracised by the teacher in the school. I was completely ignored, and it even went as far as the teacher leaving me out when he'd be giving out pens and pencils, slate, paper, anything. I was getting sly digs and rubs, and I found myself more and more isolated. It finished up that I had to get out of there. I told my father and mother about it, and they just shipped me off to my older brother in Dublin, thank God.

I was thirteen at the time, and I was absolutely delighted to get away. The first two or three months I didn't do anything much and then my brother got me into a school and I stayed there until I was sixteen in 1933. My parents and the rest of the family moved up to Dublin shortly after I left, partly because of what had happened to me, and partly because there had been redundancies in the local railway works where my father worked, so we were all together again.

I started work as an apprentice painter in a firm. I started work there at five shillings a week. We were on strike on Tuesday, and we were paid off on the Wednesday. Our mentors in the union, which was quite strong at the time, decided that the best time to go on strike was about a fortnight before the spring show, because there were a lot of cars and vans that needed painting that were going to be exhibited at the spring show. In fact, on the day before the show, all these vans emerged newly painted, because the scab labour had got in through the back gates in the night time, and we lost.

My wage for those three days was two shillings and tuppence, which I gave to my mother. I remember thinking it was marvellous to be contributing to the upkeep of the household.

My second job was going to serve my time as an apprentice motor mechanic in a garage, and I stayed there until I eventually came over here in 1941.

Five of us decided to join the airforce. It wasn't that I had any pro-British feeling at all, and I hardly knew who Hitler was. It was just to get out of Dublin and get into a fresh scene and make a new life. Don't forget there were what a quarter of a million volunteers in the British forces during the war from Southern Ireland. I had seven friends of mine killed in the war, chaps I went to school with and none of them had to join, they all volunteered.

Well if you couldn't get in the forces, the next best thing was to try and get over here to work you know. They were queuing up in their thousands in Dublin at that time to come over here. And you know it was a funny thing that Trinity College and University College in Dublin

MALE SERVANTS WANTED.

◆

JANITOR WANTED for Dublin secondary school (boys); wages, 30/- per week and small house. Address "Z 3283, Janitor," this office. 22 E

MARRIED MAN (I.O.) WANTED, SEXTON; gate lodge; extra work guaranteed.—Archdeacon Tounshend, Ahascragh, Ballinasloe. 1 D

WANTED, LAD for STABLES, able ride young horses.—D 1698, this office. 3 C

WANTED, GENERAL MAN; care horse, garden, milk; Church of Ireland.—Rev. A. A. Wilson, Kilmoe Rectory, Goleen, Skibbereen, Co. Cork. 4 F

WANTED, BOY, from 16, C. of I.; country rectory; milking, gardening, housework. Address "Z 3439, Boy," this office. 4 F

WANTED a HOUSEMAN immediately. Address "Z 3467. Houseman," this office. 4 E

YARDMAN REQUIRED, married, Protestant, good milker, work oil engine, cattle feeding, farm-work; free house, fuel, milk, potatoes, and wages 22/-. Address "Z 3455, Yardman," this office. 4 F

Irish Times

were filled up within a couple of months of the war starting with the sons of the gentry in England who were going over there to escape being called up.

I suppose there was a sense of excitement about coming over here and getting away from home. I'll always remember the indignities we had to suffer. We paraded before an American personnel officer who interviewed us in Dublin. You had to show your hands, and if there were no signs of manual work on the palms of your hands, they'd say, 'Take yourself off, we don't need you.' Well I suppose they wouldn't have been any good for what he needed. I was rejected because I'd had an operation on my eye, so I got a job over here on war work.

I came over to my eldest brother who was in Clapham. I arrived at Euston in the middle of the air raid, and I didn't know what was going on. I was here for about a week before I went to work in Walthamstow. My first job was making parts for the Spitfire planes.

I had to get digs in Walthamstow. The local landladies left their addresses at all the factories. Their husbands and sons were away at the war and they had plenty of room, so there was no difficulty finding digs. They were pleased to have you for the extra lolly I suppose, and to have a man in the house. The landladies were very understanding and very nice types. They did look after us well. There was rationing and all that. Tea and sugar were rationed back home, but the rationing in Ireland was nothing compared to here, like only one egg a week. My landlady used to keep mine and tell me it hadn't arrived, I found her son having it one morning. I didn't mind.

I remember one morning I nearly risked my life for an egg. I had to be in work at six o'clock in the morning which meant me getting up about five so I always told the landlady not to bother getting up, that I'd get my own cup of tea or breakfast going out. Well I was frying this egg, and it had been about a month since I'd had an egg. I said, 'Well I'm definitely going to have this one.' When you couldn't get them, you thought they were marvellous you know. I was frying this egg, and the next thing this crash alert came on, which meant that there was a doodlebug approaching your area, and the only way we knew that was by listening to the alerts in the factories around.

Well I waited until this doodlebug was directly overhead, and I said, 'God Almighty, well that's very near I'd better get out of here.' So I grabbed this frying pan with the egg in it, and started to run down the garden to the shelter, and as I was running down the garden I tripped because it was dark, and my egg went into the grass. That doodle bug was coming down at the time and I stayed there to pick up this fried egg. It shows you how you lose all sense of proportion. That was the Dunlop Rubber factory was hit that morning by that doodle bug in Tottenham but that was about half a mile away as the crow flies. When that doodle bug cut out you knew it was coming down and it had cut out just as I was frying my egg.

Another day I came out of work at half past two with a London chap and we waited at a bus stop for a trolley bus to take us to our digs and the bus was full so we decided we'd walk. This bus had gone on without us for about three hundred yards, but around the corner and it got a direct hit from a doodle bug, there wasn't one found alive, right on the middle of Markhouse Road in Walthamstow. If I'd got on that bus I wouldn't be sitting here. They were the sort of escapes you had. We were the first on the scene near enough to help.

There was nothing certain about them coming down anywhere. I'd just moved out of one digs into another, and a week later, the old digs was bombed in Walthamstow. They were falling short of their targets, that's why the east end of London took a much bigger hammering than other parts of London. It was the same with the rockets afterwards when they started coming down they were falling short of their targets.

It was all very exciting and you learned to live with it. The black out was the worst part, that was depressing. But it was a new way of life compared with Ireland or normal living. You had to make some adjustments. It's surprising how you can become used to things. I was only in an air raid shelter during the war about a dozen times. It was only when you thought you were in really serious danger that you went into them.

I remember climbing up the ladders right up to the top of the factory on to the roof because we heard a doodle bug in the distance, we were on night shift and eventually we were about thirty or forty of us up there and this doodle bug passed over and you could see the flames coming out of its tail. Just as it passed us, it turned and came back towards us again so there was a rush to get down those stairs, and those stairs were only wide enough to take one, the result was that two chaps fell from the roof in the crush trying to get down and had to be taken to hospital. That was the panic because it had turned back for no apparent reason.

After the war, I didn't go back to Ireland for quite a long time. I just continued living here. I'd married an Irish girl from Dublin during the war, and I brought her over here when it finished. I worked as a maintenance engineer for British Airways, and I worked for them until I took early retirement.

I've spent a lot of time in Ireland this past few years and it's changed an awful lot. The old camaraderie and doing a good turn and all that sort of thing, that's finished in Ireland now. I was surprised when I went back, an old age pensioner who lived down beside me where I was born, she's very old and she got a man to put up a little shelf for her. He charged her five pounds, and him a neighbour. And that's even more so now in Dublin, everyone has become very materialistic.

I think going into the Common Market, you know, those boom years of the seventies, it made them think that money grew on trees and they've become very greedy since, money is all that matters. You find that you have to be on the alert all the time or you'll be ripped off. I know dozens of other people like myself who go back to Ireland for their holidays now, and the one thing they say is, 'My God, they don't half rip you off over there! They do, they've got very greedy for money.

I still love Ireland the ground, the soil, the air, yes, but I've grown away from the people, a little bit. I think it's their change of attitude towards me. It's very hard to feel at home when the first question you're asked is, 'When are you going back?' You start to feel that you're on a holiday. It's brought home to you that you're on holiday, you're not really going back there for keeps.

I think every Irish person has that dream, a man anyway, to go back to Ireland to settle in their old age. It was a dream with me for ten or twelve years and that's why I took early retirement really, to go back there. I dreamed of finding a little rose covered cottage somewhere and settling down with a fishing rod and a dog and a pint of Guinness, a nice local pub somewhere, but that dream soon fades.

POSTSCRIPT: Mr. McTague has moved back to Ireland to live since this interview was recorded.

JOHN MUNALLY

I'm from County Mayo. My father was a small farmer. I lived in a country place. The nearest town was about ten miles. It was a small, little town, Ballycastle, next to the Atlantic Ocean, not far from America!

The time I was confirmed, that was a great big day. I'll remember that all my life. We were prepared for about twelve months before. We were told about it and the teacher used to come and you went through the catechism and the bible. The priest came about four times and questioned you on what you went through, and you had to know the catechism upside down and the different parts of the bible. We used to be kept in, in the evening, and God knows what time we'd get home.

Oh my God, we were up all the night before. We must be washed about twenty times. We had out hair done and we had new suits. I wore a grey little suit, the first one I ever had, and a white shirt, and I had a tie, a pair of low shoes. I think they were the first low shoes I had, because I used to have big strong boots on me. So there seemed to be an awful lot of interest put in at that time. My father and mother came to this small little church and there was two or three of us confirmed. And when the time came, the bishop only asked us very simple questions, and we were very disappointed. We thought it was a waste of time learning all we knew. I think we knew more than the bishop. That was the biggest day I had. I thought I was going to heaven the next day. I didn't feel a bit different though after it.

In our little town, there used to be house dances and every night card playing, and it was a good old life. Every Sunday night there was couple of little halls had dances in them, and that was the main attraction when we were young. It was a great community spirit, and we enjoyed it. You knew everybody and everybody knew you. But you can grow out of that. The girls we'd got to know went away to America and England, so you were lost, you had to go. You said, 'We'll follow them and we'll go somewhere too.'

We wanted more excitement. It was probably a better life we had there, but it was just a matter of being young and being told about the great things overseas. When you're young, you want to get farther afield, you want to see the world, you're never content at home. Well, there was big families in every house and a lot of them had to go. There was bad times in Ireland then too. Anyone with bits of farm or anything, they weren't doing very well, because they couldn't sell anything and there was a lot of unemployment. Most of my friends, including the young girls, came over here, and I wanted to get away. It was either here or America. I didn't exactly choose England, but the fare was smaller. It was easier; you could do it in one day.

I came over in July 1939. I was just a young lad then, aged seventeen. I knew that there was going to be a war, that it was only a matter of time. It had been in all the papers. In fact, I don't know if it was the right decision or not, but anyways, I took it. My family were a bit lonely without me, but I thought it would be a better life. I should have known better really.

Of course there was unemployment here too. It was very hard to get a job until after the war started. It was very hard to get anything in this country, there was nothing doing here.

I had a rough passage over. It was more like a cattle boat than anything else, not a very good boat really, and very small and narrow, The Princess Maud. Years after, I heard she went down and she sunk, so I says, 'It's a wonder she didn't sink then.' Everybody seemed to be sick. I hadn't much experience of being at sea except I'd been out in rowing boats; but it was nothing as bad as this was. Everybody seemed to be sick and the wind seemed to be blowing all over, and oh my God, what a horrible thing. I thought it was a nightmare journey, the first trip I went on. I was glad when it was over, anyway.

That was my first big journey, bar Dublin. I'd been a couple of times to Dublin before that. I'd been at football matches. Any time the home team'd go to Dublin, I used to go there to the football match.

It was seven and six on the boat. I got the train to Euston. And it was so crowded I don't think there was room to stand. There were a lot coming over, but there was an awful lot going back then too, going the other way. There was a lot on about war, about Mussolini and how Hitler was going mad, so there was a lot leaving England too.

They used to be coming for the harvest and men used to have their own scythes with them. They'd work on mowing hay and doing a bit of gardening, so they used to have their own material with them. They used to come just for the season at the end of July. Thousands of them used to come every year to do the harvest. They used to come too for pulling the beet. They had their own men to come to, these farmers used to have them every year after year from all parts of Ireland.

I had a job to get a job. I went to the labour exchange, but there was no job going for several days. I had a bit of money on me. I think I had around £10.

So a man gave me a job as a tea boy for a gang of men digging drains. He had no other job, and I got no money, except what I could collect off the men. You had to bring in their tea and make the tea for them and fry rashers for them, and eggs. There was only about ten or twelve men altogether. So I done a couple of weeks on that, with no cards, no money, no nothing, only just what they give you. Then I left and I got a job pulling beet for a farmer. And I stuck that for a couple of months.

Then everything changed when the war started in September. When you went into the labour exchange, oh, they gave you great questioning, and they said, 'We have jobs now.' There was plenty jobs going then. I was sent to Corsham where they were building a big underground factory for making ammunition. It was the biggest in Europe, the biggest in the world at the time. There's a real city, all underground.

So I went there and I started working for Wimpey. I was only a young fellow then. I was sent down underground. Everyone that was underground was exempt from the army. And then there was a great clamour to get underground, and there was awful arguments about who was exempt and who wasn't, and there was an awful lot of Irish going home.

The foreman used to bring all his sons down with him, and keep them down there. If you didn't suit the foreman you were up on top. And soon as you went up on top you were called up about a week after for the army. So you had to be very careful how you managed it. The foremen were like little gods. Every foreman had an awful lot of power. Then they started dishing out identity cards to everyone. If you hadn't a job underground, or essential work, they picked up everyone. Everyone had to join up.

You just travelled from job to job. You were sent to all the dangerous jobs. I remember one job I was sent to was putting in a runway down at Dover, for crashed aeroplanes which had to come in from France.

The first night I went there, there was about twenty blokes killed on the aerodrome. They were putting up a landing strip for crash landings. Oh my God, it was wicked working there. The Germans used to come in and bomb it during the day. They'd machine-gun the runway where you'd be working. So there was about twenty killed.

I did that for a week or fortnight. I think I got one pay packet. I left then, leaving my cards and everything behind me. You had no chance really. There was an awful lot killed there. So it was easy to get them sort of jobs. I knew it was dangerous when I was going, but the money was good. There was about a shilling an hour extra, on top of your wages, but they didn't tell you what was involved in it!

We'd never hear air-raid warnings. France was so near, they'd be here before they give any warning. They might blow a whistle, there was an old whistle, but it didn't tell you they could come any time and drop their bombs. So, my God, it was a bit scarey.

Then I came to London to work on repairing the bomb damage. The bombers were coming over then, every place. We used to repair houses, putting up blackouts on the windows, and putting in windows and doors, measuring them, so that the people could occupy them. We used to travel all round London.

The next thing, the flying bombs came. They were a terror altogether. The siren'd go, but you never knew where the engine would just stop. You'd hear them coming, and the next thing they'd come down and that was it. You could run, there was air-raid shelters and all that, but you had to be quick betimes. I saw some terrible damage done with them.

We were young and we tried to enjoy ourselves. You always had the crack at the weekend, and you met the boys for a drink in all the different pubs. We'd be going to the dances, the Garry Owen, the Pride of Erin, Quex Road and all these dances. There was a lot of Yanks there. Then the women, all the Irish ones then, were after the Yanks. The Yanks used to be at all the dances then; and Canadians and Australians. Oh, they used to go for the uniform, the women, I tell you.

When you hadn't got a uniform, well, if you had a steady woman it was alright, but the Yanks had the go. They had more money anyway, than we had, and they had everything. I met my wife in the Irish dance hall in Hammersmith. We were dancing away there, and I seen her dancing, and I asked her out for the Seige of Ennis and that was it! When I got her out there I asked her out for the next dance, and I asked her had she any boyfriends? And I think she said she had. But I forget it now! She preferred me to the uniforms! I think that was 1944. Oh, we used to have a falling out now and again, but we'd always get back together again, and used to go on like that. So that went on for a couple of years and we got married at the finish. And that was it.

In 1949 I came to Tottenham. We got a little house up in Tottenham, in Spigerna Road, and we were there for about ten or twelve years. Before I got married I started scaffolding, and I went around with all the scaffolding firms, and every one I could get a job with. I was scaffolding right through.

I went home to Ireland for about six years in the 1960s. The wages then were good. I went home and brought the family and all with me. I got a bit of land from the old man, but we didn't agree on things, so I said it was better I left there and came back again to England.

When you've been here for about ten, twenty, thirty years, things are so lonely and you don't meet any of your mates. Everywhere in Ireland seemed very dead at the time. I was fed up with the silence and the quietness of country life. It just seemed very strange, not meeting people, and you'd be working on your own. I couldn't settle down to nothing, so the only thing was to ramble away into some nearest town and spend the day in it! I tried to anyways, and that was about it.

I came back in 1966. I came back. And that was it; I got a flat and I brought the family over again. I knew everywhere, I knew where to get jobs, and there was plenty of work about then. Flats were easy enough. They were expensive, but they were easy enough to get.

MRS. MUNALLY

I am from West Wicklow. I came over in 1942. I was very young when my mum died. There were eight of us and I was only about three. But my older sisters, they kept house after that. Then when it came to my turn, I was the youngest girl, there was no girl after me, so I had to wait at home. I had to look after the home. I had to look after my brothers, cook the meals and do things for them. When my brother got married and brought a wife home, then I could come over here.

I got a housekeeping job in Leicester through a friend of mine from home. She was working with this lady's sister. I was there for a long time. There were only the two old people in the house. I had to do cooking and cleaning and things like that. It wasn't bad really, but the wages weren't a lot of good. But then I had my keep and all, and I used to have a couple of days off in the week. I met some nice friends around there.

Then I came to London. My sister and a few cousins were in London, so I come up to London to live. And I was working in a big munitions factory in Salusbury Road, Kilburn.

I met my husband at a dance. We went out for a couple of years, and then we got married in St. Mary's of the Angels, in Bayswater. We got a little flat with just two rooms, and a small, tiny little place to cook in. We lived there for a couple of years and then we got a place from the council. I was expecting my first baby at the time and we got this place from the council in Tottenham.

139

THOMAS O'DONNELL

I'm from County Kerry in Ireland. I lived in the country, very much in the country. Very quiet. I went to the local school, the country school. It was three miles walk morning and evening. I suppose sometimes we might be held up with rain and one thing and another. We always managed to get to it. Well, it was a small school, around a hundred pupils.

We lived in a country place and the custom there was, at that time there used to be open air dances in the summertime, at the crossroads. And we went to local houses and there'd be dances there for the country folks. There'd be dancing, make up a collection, and there'd be dancing until ten, eleven o'clock. For the dance at the crossroads, we built a concrete platform. The people used to come from at least three miles this way, different roads, and there'd be maybe six hundred people there. On a fine summer's evening there would be a couple of accordions, and maybe a fiddle, and there would be a lot of dancing. And it was nice on a summer's evening. They started about seven o'clock, and they'd have dancing until about ten, eleven o'clock, because of course there were no lights. So it was enjoyable, you know.

Then there was football and hurling. They're still very much alive today. One team of one parish might play another parish and they'd go for a county championship. There's a football field in every parish in Ireland, owned by the parish. They collected money, bought up a field and they developed it, and it's still there, handed down from parish to parish.

I come from Kerry, and Kerry's the home of Gaelic Football. The catch and kick game. Gaelic Football and hurling is a 15 man side. There's a goalie, there are six backs, two midfield and six forwards. It's played on a pitch of 140 yards long by 80 wide. Players are allowed to catch the ball and kick it with their feet. There is such a thing as goals and points. There's a crossbar, and if you put the ball under the crossbar it's a goal. But if you put the goal over the crossbar it's equal to three points. That's played in every parish in Kerry, every parish in Ireland.

They'd pick the best in the county and then field a team for the contest for the All Ireland finals and all the counties in Ireland play out that. And that's played in September, the third or the fourth Sunday in September. So there'd be a massive crowd of people in Croke Park, Dublin, around 90,000. The biggest crowd that was ever there was 92,000 in the football, but for fear of accidents they cut that down to about 76,000.

I remember the 1946 Final played in Dublin between Kerry and Roscommom. The first date was a draw, so the Final had to be replayed. And that year in 1946 it was a very wet year in Ireland, and the Government declared a state of emergency because they wanted to save the harvest and they wanted to save the peat. And de Valera at that time asked everyone to co-operate. Anyone that was working in factories, they were all supposed to go in the harvest fields, or to go on the bog to save the turf. And when that was done, and that appeal went out that night, the Council of the Gaelic Athletic Association called a special meeting, and they supported the Government in that demand. They said, 'We'll adjourn the All Ireland for three weeks', because there'd be several thousands gone from the fields that would do a lot of good to the harvest. So they'd back that.

So Kerry and Roscommon met three weeks after the draw, and the replay was — and I was at both of them — it was supposed to be the biggest match they'd ever played at Croke Park. I have seen in my lifetime well over thirty All Ireland football finals, but this was the greatest one in 1946. And I think a lot of them would agree with me. It was in a do or die effort. It was a game that everyone went into it, as if they were fighting for their lives. But when the game was over, and the whistle blew, any hard knocks that was given and taken — well it was all over. That was real sportsmanship, you know.

Kerry won the match, and of course I'm a Kerry man. It was a great celebration, a great victory for Kerry, because Kerry won it in a very sporting way. We went in, had a few drinks and all the place was happy and singing songs. We sang the Tralee song, The Rose of Tralee, because that's the capital of Kerry and that was the song on the loudspeakers in Croke Park before the Final. County songs. If Kerry played Galway, Galway Bay would be the song. If it was Dublin, they'd play Molly Malone, In Dublin's Fair City.

My father was a farmer and I helped on the farm at home. Where we come from in Kerry they went in for mixed farming: dairy cows, and store cattle, and sheep, and a few pigs. My first interest in life was in the spring of the year, because this is the time of the year when the sheep were having lambs. I used to love to go up in the morning and see a couple of lambs born. And I used to come in and say, 'Are there any lambs this morning?' And they'd say, 'There's two, there's three, there's four.' I used to go up again in the evening after school, and I used to love to see maybe twenty or thirty lambs jumping around the fields, as if they've got a fair spring. So that was my first interest in life and I still have the same interest.

I had three brothers and five sisters. I suppose you could say that I was lucky in my home. My father was able to play a concertina and melodeon, and my brother was able to play a melodeon. So, the nights were long but we didn't mind. The neighbours would come in. Well, a lot of people around were able to play music, old Irish tunes, you know. And on summer evenings we'd go along to crossroad, and on the way we were talking and so forth.

I was sixteen when I left school. I worked a few years in the farming. Then I worked for the county of Kildare producing fuel for the nation when the war was on. We were stopping in hostels. We were working in the bog, and sometimes making roads and cutting the turf and saving it, bag it and send it away all over the country. The camps were alright. There was a medical orderly in the camp, and they had a doctor of their own.

I came over here in 1948 because there seemed to be more opportunities than in Ireland. And at that time they were all coming over. Things were very good here because, even though wages were small, it was very easy to get work, it was very easy to get accommodation. But it's hard to get either of them today.

I thought that I never would get used to this life, because you see I came over here and I went into digs, and I was never in digs in my life. When I was back at home I was stopping with my people. Up in Kildare there were 24 in the camp. But coming into digs I'd never any experience of it before. I thought it was like going into prison and I took a long time to get used to it.

A few did say to me that you're going to find a big difference now going to England. So I said I won't because I was away from home, I was up the Midlands and I was up in Dublin at the matches. And I said mixing with crowds and travelling didn't come anyway new to me. So they said that part was alright, but going from home life into digs you'd be finding awful difference, which I found out for myself was true.

I'd always lived in a country place, where there was a playing pitch outside, and you could kick a ball, you could have a crack at the hurling, you could look on, or so forth. Well, when you come into city life back in Ireland, either in Dublin, Kildare or Kerry, you could always walk into a neighbour and you'd be welcome, and you could chat. But over here that seems to be different life, you know. They more or less keep to themselves here. It was a very sudden change about.

So that's what I thought most. Back in Ireland I could cross the road, go to see football, they're playing kicking the ball in the evening, and I used to pitch pennies on the road, didn't cost you nothing, you were out amongst the people. But you're over here now so it's a different kettle of fish.

I went into a factory, and I was there for a week or two; and then I went into buildings, and I stopped in the buildings ever since. There was plenty of work, but the money wouldn't be much.

When I came here first we were bringing home, I think, about £5. ten shillings after stoppages, and we had to pay for the digs out of that.

The best part of it was, when the day's work was over, you could go in and have a good sleep after working all day out in the fresh air. I could have got jobs in the factories, and the buses at the time, but I didn't fancy shift work. So I said, 'I'm going to stick to this', and stick to it I did. So I got on alright.

You got no such thing as a protection like you have today. You could be ten years working for a firm and get two hours notice, and you got no handshake. Well today you have to give notice, and you have to get notice. And you have to get payments according to your service. Well luckily I was never sacked. Well, my face must have fitted, I don't know.

I found some good digs and I was with that landlady for eight years. I think that was £2, but they were two pounds well spent. You'd get a breakfast and an evening meal, and sometimes we'd get something going out, a sandwich, you know. There was plenty of food, a warm house and good beds. At that time, round 1948, the winters here were terrible: fog, freezing fog. When we'd be out all day, and we'd be working the buildings in and out, and we'd have protective clothing, but I said to the lads, well I said, 'When I go in now, I walk into a warm home, and there'll be a good, warm meal for me there. So I look forward to it.' A lot of the lads hadn't good digs. I was lucky, I had good digs, and I stopped there and that was it.

We were sometimes sharing rooms, and when we had dinner, we were talking about hurling and football matches. If it was Monday they'd say, 'Oh, who won the matches back home?' And some of them'd have the daily paper in Irish, because it was sold here in certain places. So we'd talk about the matches, and maybe sombody would be playing some music. There was always something.

We'd go to a dance at the weekend. We mostly went to the Irish dances, because they played real Irish dances, such as The Set, and Seige of Ennis, Walls of Limerick, and the old time waltzes. The singers would sing Galway Bay and The Rose of Tralee and so on. The first Irish dance hall I went to was the Regent in Tooting Broadway. There was roughly eight or nine hundred in there at the weekends, Thursday, Saturday and Sunday night.

That dance hall went down, or something happened to it, and the next one I went to was a much smaller one, it was in Wimbledon. It was owned by the Labour Party; it was called the Morris Hall. And that was about less than half that. It would be three or four hundred, but it was very enjoyable. And of course there were bigger ones. The Elephant and Castle, The Shamrock, they used to call it. There was one in Bayswater, and there was another one in Hammersmith, The Gary Owen. There was stacks of them around. To me they were much the same. But you would of course go to the nearest one because you must always be prepared to get your transport home.

It was like being back in Ireland and that made me feel at home. They were playing Irish tunes. I say all Irish, but there was a big section of English, because they were working with Irish, and they were friends with one another. Like, men courting either ways, you know. So there was a big section of non-Irish in there as well. They were English fellows who were friends with the Irish girls, and I think they married, so that was that. I didn't go out with many Irish girls and I didn't marry myself unfortunately. Will I get married now I wonder!

CHRISTINA PAMMENT

I was born in Croom, County Limerick, on 15th December, 1929. We had what was called a labourer's cottage with an acre of land. Most of our neighbours lived in baked mud cottages, which had maybe one window, rather tiny, a fireplace, a mud floor, and that was it. And in some cottages, I can think of one particular where we were quite friendly with the family, there was a man and his wife, and twelve children in this tiny dark hall. The only heating was an open fire, and the light was from oil lamps.

My mother did a lot of the midwifery for the town. She wasn't a trained midwife, but she brought all the children into the world. And my mother always used to lay out the dead. She used to get requests from old ladies: 'Will you promise to lay me out when I'm dead?' I wasn't afraid of dead people as a child, because we often went to wakes. I remember seeing them laid out in their beds in white, and there'd be white linen, which was borrowed from somewhere or other. And the candles, and you would get a piece of sweetcake and bread and jam, and maybe the relatives would come up. It was quite exciting.

They were always telling how good that person was, and there was the usual boys who came in because there was some drink always at a wake. If there was a wake at somebody's house, you'd go up and say you were friends of the corpse. Couldn't very well dispute it!

They used to tell wonderful stories about the things the dead person did, and about the part they played in the Irish freedom struggle. There'd be stories about their schooling and about the Black and Tans. I think I learned the whole history of my homeland at wakes.

I saw an awful lot of children laid out, and heard about the little angels going to heaven. But I remember the nuns and their condolences to these mothers. They used to come up to the house to console the mother. I think infant mortality rate must have been very high, judging by all the babies I saw laid out.

My father had married late in life because he was the only son of a widow. He was forty-three when I was born, and I was the oldest child. He had been in the British army in the first world war, so he had a basic pension, I think about five shillings a week, which was often our only income. And of course because we were lucky enought to have an acre of land, he was able to grow vegetables, but meat was a great luxury. He went around in season and plucked geese, he was known as Tom the plucker, and he would sell off the down then. At Christmas he'd pluck the turkeys.

My parents did try to make something of Christmas. I remember once somebody came and I told them, 'We're having jelly and custard.' That was quite a big thing. The nuns gave the children at school presents at Christmas. The richer children got toys, but we poorer ones got boots or clothes.

I was taught entirely by nuns. I remember the nuns as being very kindly people and they gave us a good grounding in the three R's. The big problem in those days, was that you had to buy your own books. If you had a rich father, the first day of the new term he gave you five shillings — which was the average for the whole term's books — but if you were like me, you had to hope to buy your books from someone from last year, or try and study without the books. I used to be very good at school, and from the richer children I used to get an apple or a book or a penny for doing their homework. So I didn't do so bad in getting my books.

One of the highlights of the year was the Retreat. For three weeks we got good food and walked around the convent grounds and listened to sermons on hell and damnation and chastity. Sex education was unknown of course, but you were told that you must never sit in a room alone with a boy. I remember one particular retreat, somebody who obviously knew better than I did what the Father was talking about, tittered. Nobody would own up to who laughed, so we were all punished. Every one of us got six slaps.

I did well at school, but for people like me there was only one kind of job and that was domestic labour. My first job was working as a maid for three shillings a week, and that was a seventy-two hour week. The people owned a shoe shop and they had seven children. I lived at home, but I worked there from seven in the morning till at least seven at night. I'd wash the dishes, do the cleaning, make the beds and help with the cooking. I'd wait on their children, picking up after them, and I was even asked to help them with their homework.

Once someone came to the door, and the boss went to open it. I was coming down the stairs, and I heard him say, 'It's only the maid.' Another time, I was holding the baby because they'd gone out. The husband and wife came back for something, and I stayed sitting because I was holding the baby. I was told off then: 'How dare you sit down in front of the boss?'

I remember how tired I used to feel, and depressed, because I was reasonably bright and I didn't want to be doing this work. Still, they gave me food, some cast-off clothes for the family and some money. I stayed there one year, and then my father thought I was being over-worked. He could see that I was being completely worn down and that it was too much for a child to do. I got another job where I was treated a lot better, but the most I earned in Ireland was five shillings a week.

I felt there was no future for me in Ireland. My idea of my future life up to then had been to get married, have a cottage and lots of children. I already felt that marriage wasn't much of a deal. I'd watched this family where there were twelve children, and the husband was always drunk. One day he'd be beating the wife, and the next day you'd see them together, and I wondered why they stayed married when it was bringing so much misery. It was a source of great wonder to me.

I answered an advert in the paper for a hospital assistant in a private sanatorium in Virginia Water, Surrey. My father wanted me to be a nurse, but I was too young for that. I got the job, and my wage was to be telve pounds a month. Well to me that was an absolute fortune. I left Ireland in 1946 just after my seventeenth birthday. My father found me the fare, and my mother collected together what clothes she could for me in a little cardboard case. She made a bag with a string on it to wear round my neck to keep my money in. They were really upset. My father said, 'I'm giving you the return fare, so if you don't like it you can come home.'

I travelled completely alone, not like some of the girls who went in groups. When we arrived at Holyhead, I heard the first rather harsh English voice saying, 'Irish passports this way. If your passport has a harp on it, you're Irish.' Young as I was, I realised that this was a put down. I thought, I obviously know I'm Irish. I arrived at Euston, and there were all these people speaking in what sounded to me like a foreign language. And most of them didn't understand what I was saying either. Someone said, 'You've got to go to Waterloo,' so I walked from Euston to Waterloo with my bags, asking every step of the way.

I sent a telegram then to my father to say I'd got that far in one piece, because they would have been terribly worried. One thing that struck me when I did make this long journey from Euston to Waterloo, was all the bomb sites. Where was the wonderful London of the picture palace? It was dust and bombs and broken down houses and crowds everywhere. There was nothing nice at all. The whole area around Waterloo was bomb sites and dust from demolition and rebuilding.

As soon as I arrived in Virginia Water, the housekeeper told me to go into Egham and collect my ration book. I was dead beat by this time, and I didn't even know what a ration book was, but I had to take another train and try to find the place. There were some men digging up the road there, and one of them turned out to be Irish. He took me down to sort out this ration book. He told me he was living in a lodging house there, with army beds and blankets, and working a fourteen hour day in the most appalling conditions. This chap, Joe, said to me, 'You're a very nice young lady', and asked me out to an Irish dance, and he became my boyfriend after that.

I settled into the job. The conditions were good, and a lot of the other girls were Irish, and the sanatorium was in a nice place. I was helping out in the wards, and although the hours were long, I got one day off every week.

When we got our first month's pay, after duly sending half home to our parents, we bought what we called 'styles'. I remember buying a coat with my first month's wages, the first new coat I ever had. It was a lovely mulberry colour, though with my red hair it wasn't the right colour. And I bought an orange lipstick. When I think how I must have looked in a mulberry coat, an orange lipstick and red hair . . . well, I thought I was quite beautiful. Luckily people from Ireland are blessed with good skin, so I didn't need the rouge. We bought stuff called Snowfire from Woolworths for a penny, and the perfume was Ashes of Roses.

Christina with mulberry coat and ear-rings

I had a picture taken with ear-rings and everything, because I thought I looked really lovely. Don't forget that I'd been working as a maid before that, and wearing their hand-me-downs, I'd been made to feel ugly. And in Ireland, red hair was looked down on, called foxy hair, but over here it was something to be admired I got the whistle from the boys as I walked along with my long red curly hair, and I began to realise I wasn't the ugly duckling I was made to feel in my childhood.

This boy Joe took me up to London on my day off, when I'd saved enough to buy a dress. He showed me Oxford Street and a better side of London than I'd seen on my tramp from Euston to Waterloo. He took me to a great big Irish dance hall which was under a cinema in Tottenham Court Road, and I thought it was the most beautiful luxurious place I'd ever seen. It was all Irish music and Irish people and we had a wonderful time.

After about a year, I went home for a holiday. I was homesick and I missed my family. I felt great, coming home full of style. I felt I'd travelled the world because I'd been to England.

When I came back I was eighteen, old enough to start nursing, so I went to the Brook Hospital which is in Shooters Hill, South East London. That was the hospital for infectious diseases in those days. I was paid less than as a domestic in my previous job, but that was because I was training.

There was an Irish club in Woolwich, where we used to go to a dance, and I had the same Irish boyfriend, Joe. Actually I got engaged to him and sent the photo of him home to my parents. Anyway, one night I went to an engagment party of one of the girls, to an Englishman. One girl was walking home with her boyfriend, and his friend would walk me home. He was an old man, actually thirty-six years old, but that seemed very old to me then.

While he was walking me home, he told me he was a widower and he had a daughter and they lived in a prefab in Shooters Hill. Then he said would I see him again. So I used to go out and meet him, and he used to pay for me to go to the pictures, while he went for a drink, and then he'd meet me coming out, because I wouldn't go with him into pubs. Then he'd make me a cup of tea at his prefab. Then I'd tell him I had to be on duty at nine o'clock, and go and meet my boyfriend.It was a great joke with the girls, me and the old widower.

I thought he was the last person in the whole world I would ever marry. He 'd told me he never wanted to get married again, because his wife, who had died during the war, had been the perfect wife. He had one daughter who was only nine years younger than I was, so it was just friendship.

And then one day, I said to the girls, 'I'm going to marry this Englishman.' They said, 'Does he know?' I said, 'Not yet.' They said, 'You must be mad, you're engaged to Joe.' Do you want to know why I was going to marry him? Because he was a very old fashioned Englishman, like he helped me off the trams, he carried my shopping, he took my coat, all the things the Irishmen don't do, and I began to click on. He also was a very intelligent man. And so I decided, without his knowledge, that I would marry him.

My parents and everybody else was very angry. My father came over, to try to stop it, but the Englishman won him round in the end, and we went back to Limerick to get married. I married him on the 5th of October, 1948.

Unlike many of the other girls who got married from the hospital and lived in furnished rooms, I had a proper home. I had a pre-fab and a garden. It's a beautiful place, Shooters Hill, because it's all like woodlands behind. And there was only nine years between Anne, my step-daughter, and me, so we had great fun together, and for a while we had a wonderful time.

But during the years, I did find life with his friends and his relatives, very difficult. I could not relate to them at all. I didn't understand their way of life. It was completely alien to me. Every time I opened my mouth, I put my foot in it! They were very reserved. I remember going to see his sister, and she said, 'We're having our dinner.' We had to sit in the front room with a cup of tea. At home, we'd have joined in with the dinner. Don't forget there was a big age gap too, because all his family were much older than me.

I thought it was a cold and unfriendly culture. I had neighbours, but you couldn't just go in and have a cup of tea if you were lonely as you could back home. His daughter went away to school and all my neighbours were English, so soon after I married, I became very lonely.

On St. Patrick's Night, he'd let me go to an Irish dance while he looked after the baby. That was the highlight of the year. You obviously wore green, and it was packed out. There was drink going and lots of boys there, and we sang Irish songs. You felt you were home for at least one night.

Even after forty years here, I am still one hundred per cent Irish, and very much in love with my homeland. And I think it's only since I've gone back and toured it in comfort, I realise how beautiful it all is. It took my husband to point out that my house, our cottage, looked on to lovely green fields, a lovely stream running around. I have a wonderful relationship with my step-daughter, and I have five gorgeous grandchildren through her. And we get on great together. And my two sons are teachers over here, but I have never, never become an English woman. I intend to go home and settle in Limerick where my brother is. I'm very proud to be Irish.

HANNAH RAYNOR

I saw an advertisement in the paper in Ireland, in Kinsale, that's where I lived. I wrote after it and I got the job. The advertisement said they wanted an Irish girl or woman, to work as a housekeeper. Before I came to this country, I had to have a reference from a priest that I had no children while still unmarried. I was going mad because they were asking me questions like that, and I didn't approve of it. I was a very religious girl. When I was a young girl at home with my mother, she was always taking me to mass to retreats.

I came over here on the spur of the moment. I came on my own. Mrs. Cohen sent me the ticket to come and some money. This is the warning that my mother gave me: 'When you go to London be careful. I don't really want you to go to london because a lot of Irish girls go wrong in London. When you want anything, ask for it, dont take. If you're not happy there, come back home.'

I was working first for Jewish people in New Cross, Nathan and Bessie Cohen. When I came out first, I cried my eyes out, because I was lonesome after my mother. I was down in St. Saviours praying in my afternoon off work, and I was crying up at the altar rail. The Canon came over to me and said, 'Are you in trouble?' 'No Father', I said, 'but I'm lonely after me mother.' He said, 'How long are you here?' I said, 'About three weeks.' The Canon said to me, 'I'll see you here in the church on your afternoons off.' 'Alright I'll be pleased', I said, 'I'm just very lonely and I'm frightened.' After that, I had my ups and downs, but I was always in the church, the church always helped me to cope.

The Cohens had a kosher butcher's shop. I used to enjoy walking round delivering the chickens, already cooked, from the shop. I did domestic

COOKS AND DAIRYMAIDS WANTED.

BALLSBRIDGE—COOK GENERAL WANTED; wages £40; two other maids kept; daily Cook might suit; enclose copies references.—D 1699, this office.

COOK GENERAL WANTED; 30 miles Dublin, country town; modern house; other maid; small family; good wages, reliable girl. Address "Z 3378, Cook General," this office. 31 C

COOK GENERAL and HOUSE PARLOURMAID or GENERAL REQUIRED for country about January 10th. Write, sending references, to Mrs. Fitch, Lismehane, O'Callaghan's Mills, Co. Clare.
1 F

COOK GENERAL and HOUSE PARLOURMAID WANTED, aged 20 to 25; very nice post; good wages; health, cleanliness and efficiency essential; Protestants. Apply fully to Mrs. Norman, "Highcroft," Parkside avenue, London, S.W.19. 2 D

COOK GENERAL WANTED, Irish family; two adults, two young children; London suburbs; interview Dublin; salary £45; first class references required.—D 1736, this office. 3 E

COOK GENERAL and HOUSE PARLOURMAID WANTED, age 20 to 35; very nice post; good wages; health, cleanliness and efficiency essential; Protestants. Apply fully to Mrs. Norman, Highcroft, Parkside avenue, London, S.W.19. 3 E

EXPERIENCED DAILY COOK GENERAL REQUIRED; must be good cook; two in family; North side.—D 1602, this office. 31 C

EXPERIENCED COOK GENERAL REQUIRED; 2 in family; good cooking essential; very comfortable house and good wages for capable person.—D 1601, this office. 31 C

EXPERIENCED COOK GENERAL; family two; good wages, good outings; no rough work.—D 1700, this office.

GOOD COOK GENERAL WANTED; £30. Apply 18 Northumberland road before 1 o'clock or

Irish Times

work in the house and in the shop. I used to scrub the meat blocks, pluck the chickens and all. I was good at getting company into the shop. I was friendly with all the Jewish people. They were the best people I ever worked for.

I liked to do the cooking. The Cohens were very fond of soup, sweet and sour borscht, made from beetroot. I used to love that. They used to cook the chicken on a Friday. They had their dinner early on that day because it was their sabbath. Mrs. Cohen would say to me, when I was delivering the chickens, 'Don't be long Hannah, because Shabbas comes in at half past three.' I used to eat with them, especially on Shabbas. I used to wear brown and white, and then if there was any people coming to dinner, black and white. On those occasions I would wait at table, and I would enjoy that. When the Cohens had a high dinner, on what they called High Holy Days, I used to be dressed up to the knocker. Very proud of myself I was then.

They took a great interest in me, and they acted as a mother and father to me. I was like a daughter to the Cohens, they had no trouble with me.

My mother had photographs of Mr. and Mrs. Cohen on the wall at home in Kinsale. I'd sent her the photographs. Jack, my brother, wrote back to me, 'Why ever did you send those photos, the priest came in and he didn't like it. He didn't approve of them.' Jack told me the priest had said to my mother, 'Is that who your daughter is working for?' So my mother said, 'Yes, Father, it is where Hannah is working.' And she had to take them down. I think it was for a religious reason he said that. Father Murphy was his name and he was fond of the bottle. My mother sent the pictures back.

The Jewish people have their Sunday on Saturday, but my Sunday was religious too, so I never worked. I said to Mrs. Cohen, 'I'm a very religious woman.' I had a row with her over the religion. I told her I wouldn't work Sundays because I wanted to go to Church. She said, 'Why didn't you tell me that in your letter.' I said, 'Well there's an easy thing for that ma'am, I can still go back home.' Well now, I had a friend who was working for the Jewish minister in New Cross Road, and I went and consulted him. He said I was right that I claimed my Sunday for the religion.

One time I was looking out for this man who was supposed to come in for the dinner, and I found him standing praying away behind the door with his keppel on (that's a little cap they wear) and he was a nice tall young man. 'Good Yomtov', I said to him, which is a greeting. He finished his prayers and he sat talking to me. He said to me, 'Where do you come from?' So I said, 'I come from Ireland and I'm proud of it!' So he says, 'My mother and father are Irish Jews from Cork City!' 'Good Gracious me', I said, 'Isn't that lovely!' and I was praying to the Lord myself. I told him that my mother used to deal with a Jewish man in Ireland. My parents had a clothes shop in Kinsale and they used to travel around a lot, and we used to have clothes off him, and pay him so much a week. This young man by the door man was just very religious. He told me that when he was a young boy, something happened to his parents. He got very lonely because he had no-one, no-one at all. I sent him to the Jewish Minister. He went down there and I believe they found a place for him there in one of their own synagogues.

My Governor, God bless her, Bessie Cohen said to me, 'Don't go in any dark places.' This was a warning because I was quite young. She'd say, 'Keep out in the lights, and don't go anywhere away from the lights, otherwise you'll get into trouble.' There were a lot of girls come out from Ireland, and they did get into trouble with boys. There was one customer who had an Irish girl working for her. And this Irish girl was a bit funny after boys. This girl did get into trouble. My missus told me that she was going to be transported home. There was no welcome for her in Ireland. She was a Cork city girl. She was too young to be here because she didn't understand the rules of the world, I call it. What kept me safe and sound was prayers.Thank God, and his Blessed Virgin Mother the Lord's taken me all the way through up to today.

I'll make you laugh now. I went to the pictures and I came out of the pictures at New Cross, and I was standing underneath the lampost outside my house. A young man stole a kiss off a my face. When I went in, Mrs. Cohen said, 'Hannah, don't ever do that again, because its not ladylike.' I'd only just met him, and his name was Charlie. He phoned me up next night. He was working in the greengrocer in Catford. He used to shout after me, you know. He'd call out to me and I used to tell him off. I lost my Irish temper. I called him everything. 'Go home and shout after your mother, and don't mind shouting after me in the street!' He started laughing and spitting at me, and I didn't like it. But I will say this, he was a nice decent boy when I got in his company. He apologised then.

Charlie and I never went to dances, I kept away from dancing. We used to go to the pictures. He used to come down to the shop to see me, and

when the Gov'nor went out, Charlie'd have a cup of tea and a talk with me and that was it. We got married at St. Saviours, Lewisham. The Cohens came to our wedding, and the Jewish Minister's wife came in to see me getting married! My mother never came to England because she was too fat!! I used to go home as often as I could, but when she died, I gave up.

I had my wedding breakfast in Ethel's house, that was Charlie's elder sister, in Hither Green. We went to Southend for our honeymoon. We had a week in a flat behind the gasworks. His mother and his sister gave me their blessing. His mother said she didn't mind him marrying an Irish girl, providing I was a good wife to him. And I was up to now! We're quite happy.

We had a flat in Tanners Hill, near New Cross, and we used to have half a chicken for our dinner on a Saturday from the Cohens. I carried on working for them for a long time after I was married, right up to the war years. I went down to see them one Shabbas morning, and when I went down she was killed sitting in a chair, and he was killed sitting in a chair. It was a direct hit.

157

KITTY THOMPSON

I'm from Kilmaganny in County Kilkenny. There were five of us in our family. The best part was when I was a little one, before my mother died. We used to go around the fields and play at home and pick flowers. We used to play, and I've never heard anyone saying it, but we used to call it Cabby. We used to go out in the fields, and a lot of people would throw out broken things like cups and saucers or jugs, and we used to put it all around in the grass, and we'd make it look very nice, all the different colours. Just that, and we used to call it cabby, and I used to love doing that.

But then I couldn't go out a lot because my mother was ill you see. She wasn't well for about three or four years before she died. She'd be up and down in bed and you know when you're young, you'd want to go out and play. I used to have to clean all the place, and I was only very young. She couldn't do it because she was ill, and I used to have to water the flowers, make the bread, everything.

We were always outdoors, especially in the summertime. We used to always love to go in the fields. They used to have a lot of rivers in the fields. We used to take our shoes off, walk in the river, you know, when it's a real hot day, walk in the river. We used to love to do that. Or if we had a storm, we used to go along the roads and watch the steam come up. You know, a storm, a big shower in the summer time, we used to love to walk on it.

And I remember my mother used to be telling me off because you catch cold that way. But we still done it. And then in the winter, we used to go up the hill, you know in the real frost on the hill road, and we used to go up to the top and slide down, and the moon'd be shining and we'd stay there for hours playing. But then after my mother got sick, I couldn't do anything . . . the others were all out playing, but I couldn't, being the oldest, I had to stay in with me mam.

Times were very bad when I was a child in Ireland. Christmas time, they'd fill your stocking up with cinders and just an orange on the top. When you're young and you see other children getting things, it made you feel very disappointed. I remember if my mother used to boil an egg for my dad, he used to take the top off for me. If he had another egg, he'd give the top to my sister. They couldn't afford to give an egg to all the children.

We mostly ate porridge which we didn't like much, and then we'd have sandwiches to bring to school with us and a bottle of milk. In the evenings we'd have potatoes and cabbage, and sometimes some boiled bacon. And of course there was the wholemeal bread. I used to watch my mother make the bread. I was so small I couldn't reach up to the table, so I had to stand on a stool. I used to put the flour in a basin, mixed with salt, add the sour milk and mix it all up. We'd flatten in out and put it on a very heavy steel pan and put that on the fire, leave it for a while and then turn it.

I made my first communion when I was seven. Me mam's sister was living in America and she sent me a lovely beautiful frock and I was so proud of it. It was all lace, a lace cape and a veil, shoes and all, I got the whole set. I felt so lovely and it was the first time I ever had anything really nice.

They were very strict. You had to get an older girl to teach you the catechism, and you had to go over it with her every evening after school. You had to learn it off by heart. And then the morning you make your first communion, the priest shall ask you whatever question he wants to ask you, and you had to know it all off. It would be a crime if you were to make a mistake, but it was nice you know.

St. Patrick's Day was a great day in Ireland. We used to go up in the fields and pick the shamrock. Everybody'd go to mass in the morning and then there'd be processions. All the children used to walk in the parades. Everybody had to wear green, my mother knitted a green frock for me and I used to wear ribbons in my long hair, green ribbons, it had to be green. It would be a good day.

I was the oldest girl and when my mother died, I had the care of the others. I used to make the bread for us all. There was five of us and my dad was going to work, going round the countryside selling groceries in a van, and he couldn't cope with us. He put my three brothers in a school in County Tipperary, and my sister and I went into a convent in Kilkenny.

We had to wear a uniform there, navy in winter and check frocks in the summer. Once you went into a convent in those days, you were there till you left. You didn't go home for the holidays.

I stayed there from thirteen to sixteen and then I went to work in the public laundry belonging to the school. We used to get about one shilling and sixpence a week, but you had your keep. We did all the washing and ironing there and we worked very hard, long hours. You'd start at eight o'clock in the morning, and sometimes if you were very busy you'd have to go on till eight o'clock at night. All the people working there were those children who'd been bought up in the convent. There was no social life and we weren't allowed out. In the evenings we'd have the wireless on, and you'd talk with your own friends, make clothes.

You had to leave at eighteen, so the nuns got me a job in Dublin in a big hospital run by the same order of nuns, the Sisters of Charity. They put me on a train, my very first time on a train, and there were two nuns to meet me at the station and we went by taxi to the hospital. I worked there in the laundry. The other girls were mostly girls who'd been brought up in other convents round the country.

We could go out and go round the shops and look at everything. Dublin was a lovely place. Cleary's in O'Connell Street was my favourite shop. We used to go and buy little things there. We hadn't the money to buy a lot, but I remember getting a lovely black coat with a fur collar and a belt for ten shillings.

We had to be in at nine o'clock so we didn't get to dances because they didn't start till about nine. We used to go to the pictures often, or just go for a walk around the town. The nuns were responsible for us and they'd tell you off if you were late.

The football used to be very exciting you know, my friend and I used to go to Croke Park, Dublin. We used to go everytime there was an All

Kitty outside Cappagh Hospital near Dublin with friends in 1932.

Ireland, especially when Kilkenny were playing because that's where I was from. It used to be good. Oh yeah, we used to love it. We'd just go and have a cup of tea after the match. I never drank when I was young. Well, I never seen drink in the house. We'd just have a cup of tea, and then we'd get talking in the cafe. All the blokes would be in there after the match and you know when you're young they'd be tryin to chat you up.

Oh, we'd be very disappointed, we'd be so disappointed when Kilkenny'd lose you know, because they were a great team at that time, years ago.

We used to look forward to St Patrick's Day. Everybody comes out on St Patrick's day to watch the parades. And they had bands all around the town. On St. Patrick's Day, if you told the sister you were going to be out late, you could go to a dance. Oh it used to be good. We used to do ourselves up for that. At that time, I didn't use make up, but you would buy a new frock for St Patrick's day, even when you got older. Yes, always green, you had to buy green on St. Patrick's Day, green and yellow, mostly green. You'd wear something in your hair, a green slide or a ribbon. Oh yeah, and we used to have the shamrock. It was a great day, St Patrick's Day in Dublin.

Kitty in 1932, Phoenix Park, Dublin with friends.

I would buy a new frock for St Patrick's Day. It'd always be green, and a green slide in your hair. You'd go early, but there wouldn't be many men there, they'd always go into the pub first, and then when they'd be a bit merry they'd come into the dance hall. We used to do the Irish dancing, the Lancers, where you do a lot of swinging around you know. It used to be good.

I came to England in February 1939. A friend of mine, Nora, had got a job over here in Hampstead as a housemaid. She got me a similar job in a guest house nearby. I was a bit nervous coming over on my own, but my grandmother said to me, 'Just follow the crowd.' There were people there from the job to meet me at Paddington Station. I got more money here. One pound ten shillings I was getting here, and I thought that was great. I just helped with the beds, and cleaning the stairs, and did a bit of ironing for the landlady, just housework really.

I took a job then with my friend in the Royal Masonic School in Bushey, Hertfordshire. I had to give in my notice, and the lady I was with, she was very annoyed that I'd come from Ireland, you know, she'd given me the job and I was leaving her. She didn't like it you know, but I said I liked laundry work, I was always used to it you see. The school was very good, I liked it there. I stayed a long time there. I was in the laundry, and that was what I really liked.

KITCHEN, LAUNDRY, ETC., WANTED.

TWO sisters or friends as KITCHENMAIDS, outside London, immediately. 'Phone **91708.**

After six months, I met my husband through the friend that got me the job over here. He was an Englishman working in a hotel, but when the war started he joined the Royal Artillery. They never knew when they were going to be called up to go out abroad. And he said to me, 'Wouldn't it be a good idea to get married because I could draw the allowance.' Well, I didn't really want to get married so quick, but I said yes. I got married on May 11th 1940. It was a hurried up wedding because during the war you had to get a special licence, and he was expecting to go abroad at any moment. My friend Nora was a witness and her boyfriend was the best man. We came back to London for a week of honeymoon and of course I fell for my oldest daughter.

Kitty with her daughter in Kilkenny

I went back over to Ireland when I was pregnant. I wanted to stay in London but I couldn't get a place, so I went back home. My dad was still alive and he had a house out there, so I stayed with him over there. I had a good father, he looked after me, I had my allowance you see, oh that was good, the money.I didn't mind it. It was different, really different from over here. It was only a little village, you know. Everybody knew one another. Over here you get used to traffic, and you feel lonely without it. I felt lonely in Ireland.

On May 10th 1942, my oldest daughter was born, and my husband was still out abroad. He didn't see my eldest daughter till she was a year and nine months when he came back on leave. She was walking, and I hadn't seen him all that time. I got pregnant then with my younger daughter.

He had to go back again and then he got wounded. He was discharged then, so he came back to Ireland again for a few weeks. Then he came back to England and he got a job in a hotel. He tried everywhere to get a place for me, but he couldn't find anything, especially as we had children. They wouldn't want you at all. So my younger daughter was born in Ireland and we stayed over there quite a while because he couldn't get a place.

In the end I came back and I stayed with my brother with my two children. My husband stayed in his live-in job because my brother hadn't room for him because he hadn't a big place, you know. In the end, we found one room, at a low rent, but I didn't like it. There was a double bed in it and we set up mattresses on the floor for the children. We had a dressing table and a wardrobe, a little table and chairs, and a weeny little kitchen where we had a cooker, but you had no privacy and my husband got fed up.

My husband was a changed man after he left the army. He couldn't settle down to married life, especially with the children. You have to have great patience with children, and he didn't have them when he was younger because he'd been away in the war. He didn't want any responsibility. He was very secretive. I often asked him where he was working, because I thought I should know in case anything happened, but he wouldn't tell me. He couldn't settle down, so he left. One morning, when I got up, he was gone. It was 9th December 1950. I didn't know where he went, and I have never seen him since.

I went to see the priest in Clapham Common to ask for some advice. He said, 'I think your best plan is to get the girls into a school where they'd

165

be looked after and educated.' I didn't like to do it, but I had to. I didn't want them or myself to be a burden to my brother or to anyone else. So that's what happened.

Well, I had no money, and I had to go back and work in the laundry at the school where I'd been before in Bushey. The matron was pleased to have me back because I'd got on well with everyone there. The children went off to be boarders at a convent school in Littlehampton. In the holidays, they used to stay with my brother. He was very good and looked after them, and I used to go down and see them a lot but it all cost money. I paid their fees out of my wages, so I never had anything for myself much. I remember when I couldn't even buy myself a pair of stockings. They were hard times.

We had a few Christmases with my brother, and we used to club together for that. When she left the convent, my oldest daughter came to work with me at the school in Bushey. They paid fairly good money and you got good food and your keep.

In the end, I came back to Clapham and I got a council flat. But when I got broken into I was nervous then on my own, so I got into sheltered accommodation. It is very nice here. I can go to bed and I don't have to worry about anyone breaking in my door. There's a warden here, and there's no noise, so you can get a good night's sleep. I'm happy now. I'm on my own, but I'm on the phone and my family all ring me up, and I can ring them whenever I want. I like going to Ireland for holidays, but I'm happy here because my children and grandchildren are here, and all my brothers.

BRIAN WATTERS

I come from Collon in County Louth. The town was settled by an Anglo-Irish family, and the population was roughly half Catholic and half Protestant. There were just as many children who went to the Church of Ireland Protestant school as went to our national school. My father was a shoemaker by trade and he made boots and shoes for the gentry. His father and grandfather did the same but my father wouldn't let any of his family work at it. He said it was a dying trade, that people didn't want handmade shoes or boots because they bought them at the shops cheaper than he could make them.

When we were going to school we had a very caring schoolmaster and his wife was a teacher too. Any of the children that were bright or showed some interest, they put them forward for examinations to become teachers or civil servants. This teacher would give extra lessons morning and evening and he wouldn't charge for it. He got the application forms and did the paper work himself, applying for these jobs for the children. During the time I was at school eleven pupils left to go into teacher training. They wouldn't have had a ghost of a chance without the commitment of this marvellous schoolteacher and his wife. Some of the protestant children came to our school to get the extra tuition.

I tried for the examination to go to teachers' training college and failed. I passed most of it except arithmetic. The reason why I didn't pass on that was that I used to get a younger brother of mine to do my work for me. He was very good at figures and I wasn't. So I left school at fifteen. There were not a lot of opportunities, all I had to look forward to was shop work. I used to scan the daily paper for advertisements for young people to 'serve their time' as apprentices to the grocery trade or draperies or something like that. I must have answered dozens and dozens of advertisements but I got nowhere. This went on for one whole winter. Eventually I got work and went to serve my apprenticeship in a little place called Nobber, County Meath. I got no pay, nothing at all for two years except my keep.

Then I had a stroke of luck. A chap I went to school with, inherited a grocery business when his brother died, and he asked me to go and work for him. We weren't like employer and employee. We were just like friends. He and I were pretty close and we used to go round together in his little motor car. Then he suddenly decided to get married, which was no good to me at all. That put the kybosh on my social life.

I finished with the grocer's shop and they all thought I was mad to be leaving it. As they shook hands with me they said I shouldn't go and that they were sorry to let me go, but I had made up my mind anyway. I packed up the grocery business and came over here. I had a brother over here in England already. He was an occupational therapist in Chester, and he'd been on at me a long time to come over. I answered an advert and got the job without an interview.

I had to scrape the fare up. There was a lot of resistance at home to my going. It's a thing that I'll never really forgive my father for although he's been dead for the past forty years, he never asked me how I was going to get there. You see I used to hand my wages over to him, even to the age of twenty-three, I wasn't allowed to just put my wages in my pocket. The Saturday night before I left I handed him the wages as usual and he gave me five shillings back. He never mentioned my leaving and I didn't either.

The week before I left my mother went up to Dublin with me and we bought a suit. She was a very fashion conscious woman. She was a bit proud, so she wouldn't go to a local place. She had to go to Dublin to get me kitted out and all the rest. My father didn't talk about it at all. He was a very cautious careful man as regards money. He never had much money and what he did make he saved. He had a chest at the top of the stairs which he used to put all his money in. He never let any of it out except to the oldest boy in the family who inherited the whole lot, the house, the furniture, the heirlooms, the money, oh the rows we had over all that.

Well back to my journey. There were thousands of people coming here at that time to work. I got in the long queue and got my visa stamped and boarded the boat to Holyhead. I was going to work at Cholsey mental hospital near Reading. They were very short staffed and they were delighted to see me. I was given a blue serge uniform, a belt and a bunch of keys. It was rather like a policeman's uniform with a peaked cap.

The next morning I was on the ward. That was the twenty fourth of June, 1941. I had to start from scratch with no training. I had to keep an eye on the patients, take them out to the courtyards for recreation and take them out on the sports field if they were good at cricket or anything like that. Then you had to see that they had their meals, medications and so on. Some of the wards had seventy beds, and the first thing you had to do in the morning was start making beds. The deputy charge nurse taught me that and I didn't take long to pick it up. I loved to see all the beds done up, that was the most important thing, never mind about the patients!

It was very sunny warm weather. The river Thames used to run along the bottom of the garden and we'd walk along the river bank to the pub, and that's where I met my wife.

I had a couple of memorable experiences at Cholsey. It very often happened that you had to go on night duty without any prior warning, and one night I saw that I was on the acute ward. The chap who was on this ward, a very nervous fellow, met me and he said, 'I wouldn't like to be in your shoes, going on there.'

Well I got quite windy about this because there were about fifty patients and they were all violent. The door was locked and you were on your own. When I went on they seemed fairly quiet so I got my book out, sat by the fire and started reading. Suddenly, one of the fellows was out of bed, he raked the fire over, got some coal and put it on and then got back into bed. I never budged, I just sat there with my book. Well that was alright. Then at three o'clock in the morning I heard a noise behind me. I was petrified. I looked straight forward and I saw the shadow of a man standing right behind me, and I thought, 'This fellow's going to catch me by the throat or something.' But actually it was this harmless old patient who always carried a button around, and he was passing this button from one hand to the other. And I'd thought that I was going to be strangled! That was my first night.

I had my ups and downs, and there were a few violent scenes. There was a very disturbed young Irishman, a labourer from Donegal in the padded cell, and the chap who carried up his breakfast put it on a little table outside. He and I were both going to go in to him because you weren't supposed to go in on your own, but this chap got called away. There was a row going on down the corridor, lots of broken crockery, so the chap had to rush out in case one of his cronies was getting a hammering. I thought, 'There's no point in waiting any longer', so I took the plate of porridge in one hand and the cup of tea in the other, and I went in. Well, the porridge was all over me, and he was naked, he hadn't got a thing on. I couldn't do anything, there was porridge everywhere and we were rolling round this padded cell, and he was strong, oh he was strong! He gave me a fair good hiding. Eventually I got out and that was one lesson I learned: I didn't go in on my own in future to one of those places.

I got on well with all the staff there, English and Irish. One of them made a date for me with Teresa, who was an Irish nurse in the hospital. I'd noticed her alright, but I thought this was a bit of a liberty. Anyway, I went along with it. We weren't courting very long. We got married in March 1942. Teresa was only nineteen, so she had to have her mother's permission to marry. We sent the form over for her mother to sign, but she wouldn't give permission and she sent it back, so Teresa signed it herself! We got married in the local Roman catholic church, and had a very nice wedding breakfast in a hotel. We had chicken, even though it was wartime, and that was very unusual. My brother was there and a crowd of our friends from the hospital.

Then it was back to work, it was strict segregation. The main corridor was right down the hospital. The females that side and the males that side. No way could you go over there. But we did have a short honeymoon first. We went up and stayed with a brother of my mother's, a jolly old character who worked in the buildings. That was our annual leave, at the end of that week we only had a couple of bob left to do us until our next payday.

TERESA WATTERS

I'm from County West Meath in the Midlands of Ireland. I come from farming stock. I was born in 1922, and there were five of us, three brothers and two sisters. My father was fifty-three when he married, and my mother was thirty-three. She was a very hard woman. She idolised the boys and she didn't have any time for the girls. The boys were dressed to perfection, in clothes that were advertised in the fashion pages of the national paper, but my sister and I were just pushed into the background.

From the age of five we were helping on the land. We had to go down with a bucket and pick up stones where a field was being got ready for a meadow which would need to be mowed. We had to go down all those long fields thinning out the turnips. I was a bit delicate as a child, always very very pale, but we girls still had to do a lot more tasks than the boys. When I came in in the evening, after working out on the land, I had to deal with the pigs. There were always a lot of pigs around, sows with litters, and at one time there were forty-two pigs around the house. You had to get a haul of potatoes from the garden, wash them, chop them, and fill up the pigs' pots. The boys were allowed to go off to pitch and toss with their friends, but not my sister and me. So at a very early age, I must have been about ten or eleven, I decided that a farming life was not for me.

I lost a lot of time at school from having to help looking after the home. I left school at an early age because my mother was ill. She had been thrown from a horse. She was a great woman for driving. We used to have a horse and trap, and she liked stylish horses. She drove very fast and this horse ran away, it took fright, and she was thrown out of the trap and was hopped along the road for I don't know how long. She was in bed then for about two years, because she was very ill. I had to take over the running of the household, make the bread, do all the shopping.

We always killed our own pigs, so there was mostly fried or boiled bacon, cabbage, swedes . . . there was no shortage in our house. But my mother was always shouting at me from upstairs. She knew by the sounds in the kitchen what I was doing, so she knew if I was doing something wrong. She would know if I went into the parlour where there was sugar and things. I was shocking for sugar. I could blend up a half cup of sugar with water and eat it. I used to get a clump on the ear for that if she caught me.

My hardest job was turning a feather tick, that's a mattress about eighteen inches thick. I'd have to get my mother out of bed and sit her on a chair, and turn this tick, and get the feathers out to the different corners. If I didn't do it properly, I got a very hot ear. She was a wicked woman. After I got married, my husband, he loved her, but then he was a man, and she gave him the best treatment!

We used to have the national paper, the Irish Independent, and there were advertisements for sanatoriums and hospitals over here in England. From an early age I'd been scanning the paper and hiding it, hoping that one day I would be able to apply to one of those. When I was old enough, I applied to the Fairmile Mental Hospital in Cholsey, near Wallingford, Berkshire. They sent me the application form and I filled it in, saying I had been educated at a convent. I hadn't, but there was a bit of status about the convent education. I had to get the parish priest to sign it, but that part of the form wasn't filled in at the time when he signed it.

My mother had to sell a pig to pay for my fare. It was a big fat pig, so that bought the suitcase as well. I took some underwear and a rainmac, a tweed coat, a pair of flat shoes and black stockings, all in the one small suitcase, brand new. They would provide the uniform. We lived five miles from the nearest town, Edgeworthstown in County Longford, and I had never been on a bus or train. I cycled to the bus, and left the cycle for somebody else in the family to pick up. There was a chap playing the accordian on the bus and I thought it was all marvellous.

I arrived in Dublin on 18th January, 1939 and I was quite excited. I am one of those people who is never lost, so I found my way to Dun

Laoghaire and there I bought a postcard to send home. It was a picture of a ship and I can remember to this day what I wrote: 'Ready for off now, cheerio, Teresa.'

I was travelling for twenty-four hours, and at about four o'clock on a lovely sunny afternoon I walked up to the hospital at Cholsey. I was kitted out with a uniform in the matron's office. It was striped, with pearl buttons and collar. I was given a room to myself, with a jug and washbasin, and it seemed like a very good home to me.

I went on duty at seven o'clock the next morning. I had no idea what a mental hospital would be like at all. I thought the patients would be in bed, but they weren't. You had to dress the people on the ward, but I found I was able to cope. We had to make the beds with an envelope finish, and the seventy-two beds were all lined up exactly. I had to give out the crockery and the meals, and we were given lectures twice a week. There were different grades of wards. Ward six was where all the tyrants were. They used to throw the crockery around, so they all had tin mugs, unbreakable. When you are there in that situation, you accept what goes on, and one day runs into another.

We were paid fifteen shillings a week, and I sent my first pay home. We had one and a half days off a week and we used to go into Reading on the train. On one occasion, I missed taking my day off because one of the night staff didn't show up. I got thirty shillings for that so I went and got my lovely wavy hair permed and I was very pleased with that. Of course I couldn't manage the perm myself, and it went all frizzy, so I had to go for a marcel wave for a half a crown, and that helped the perm until it grew out again.

There was an outbreak of diphtheria at the hospital and I contracted it. I had to go to an isolation hospital, which was in the middle of Wallingford Park. I was six weeks there. You had to lie on boards underneath the mattress. I saw some children die there. It was all very sad. But a nurse there used to read the cards, and I used to be wishing for this lovely boyfriend. And when I came out of there, I met up with this airman from Cambridgeshire, and I went out with him for over a year. He had a large motorbike, we used to go everywhere. He was very handsome, with fair hair, blue eyes. Anyway, one night, I suddenly decided: 'Well, if this chap is not a Catholic and he's not Irish, then I couldn't take him home.' And I thought I would be sort of cut off from home. So I decided that was it. I packed this chappy up and I had

Teresa Watters in uniform at Cholsey